The Rich Don't Pay Tax!

...or Do They?

Examining who really pays US income tax, both personal and corporate, and how to avoid the largely un-seen, disastrous effect of the disparity in taxes, on the US economy.

by John Gaver

Published by Allegiance Books

Table of Contents

Preface

This book is about three issues:

1. Which income groups pay what amount of the personal income tax load,

2. The unseen threat this presents for our economy, and

3. What we can do about it.

To properly address these issues, this book is divided into three parts, each part focusing on one of these issues.

In Part 1, we'll be dealing with raw IRS data and I'll be drawing your attention to certain relationships that exist within that data. I'll also be making points that will be of significance in addressing the very important issues that will be presented in Part 2. This is where we'll deal with who really pays what amount of personal income tax.

Then, in Part 2, I'll explain why the issues that were brought up in Part 1 are of such critical importance. This is where you'll see the effect of the "Law of Unintended Consequence," as it applies to taxes and why these unintended consequences represent such a threat to our economy.

Finally, in Part 3, I'll present a set of goals designed to target the problems that we've identified and follow that with a viable and simple solution to address these goals in a fair and equitable manner, without raising taxes on any law-abiding citizen and without more deficit spending.

Caution: As you read Part 1 of this book, you may get the impression that I am biased toward certain income groups. That is not the case and it is not my intent, as you will learn, in the Part 2. It's just that, due to the nature of the IRS data, it's very difficult to present the points that need to be made, without sounding somewhat biased. But if you look closer at the IRS data that's presented here, you'll realize that the data speaks for itself.

What I'm actually doing in Part 1, is making several very important points that you'll need to thoroughly understand before you get to Part 2. It's not that those points are difficult to understand. It's just that they're not obvious in the data, until you examine the data closely. Also, the solid facts presented herein probably differ substantially from what you've been told by the media and the politicians.

So, I'll be going into some detail to not only present solid and easily understood proof, but to create the "understanding" of what's going on, so you'll be better able to comprehend the importance of the critical issues presented in Part 2.

OK. So what does all that mean? Well in plain terms, it means that I'm going to lead you, step by step, to an inescapable conclusion.

I just want you to understand that while this book is largely about taxes, it's also about the **effect** of those taxes. It isn't so much about whether or not you or I like the situation, as it is about **solutions** that are fair to everyone.

So if something that I say in Part 1 or 2 makes you angry, it's to be expected. In fact, most people who learn about the unintended effects of our current tax system do get angry,... at first.

Just be careful not to get too angry. After all, I did tell you that I'm leading you to an ending that you can't escape. In the end, you may come to the conclusion that some of your anger may have been misdirected.

Of course, I wouldn't be so crude as to create a gloom and doom scenario, without providing a viable solution. As you'll see, this nation is facing some serious problems, of which many outside of government remain blissfully unaware. In fact, many in government seem oblivious to these problems, as well.

But interestingly, many of these problems can be easily solved within a rather short period of time, **IF** we act soon. As you'll see, our window of opportunity is shrinking, so we can't delay long.

In short, after I've laid out the tax facts in Part 1 and defined the problems that those facts create in Part 2, I'll use Part 3 to show you a viable solution that many economic experts already agree, would go a long way toward resolving all of the aforementioned issues.

Part 1:

Who Really Pays Tax?

1. Politics, the Media, Taxes, and Truth

"The rich don't pay tax!"

How many times have you heard that statement?

When you hear that, what do you think?

Don't you wonder how much more you're having to pay in taxes, because a bunch of greedy rich people pay little or no tax?

Doesn't it make you angry that the rich are the ones who get all the tax breaks, while you get no breaks at all?

Doesn't it make you think we should soak the rich?

Well if you answered yes to any of those questions, you know why the left and the media say it so often.

But there's just one problem with that statement.

It's a LIE.

That's right. It's a bald-faced lie.

But how can it be a lie? Everyone knows that the rich don't pay tax.

The media tells us all the time, about how rich people use tax breaks that aren't available to lower-income taxpayers, to get out of paying their fair share of income tax. In fact, they even tell us about specific cases, from time to time.

Furthermore, every time Congress talks about taxes, we hear all about tax cuts for the rich, but we never hear about tax cuts being for the poor or middle class.

With all of this talk about the rich not paying tax and getting more and more tax breaks, how can it all be a lie?

Repetition

It's actually pretty easy to understand. You see there's a maxim in politics and the media that states, *"Repeat a lie often enough and loudly enough and it will eventually take on the aura of truth."*

If you believe that the rich don't pay tax or even that they don't pay their fair share, then you've been deceived by this old political tactic and I'm about to prove it to you.

I'm not going to ask you to believe me. Instead, to prove my point, I'll show you the actual numbers, from the IRS, that prove that not only do the rich pay far more than their share of tax, based on income, but that the amount of tax that the rich pay has been going up rather steadily since President Reagan left office.

Left wing politicians pandering for votes from those who are largely poor have found a gold mine of votes in their *"soak the rich"* propaganda. They tell their lower-income or poor constituents, *"The rich don't pay tax, but if you vote for me, I'll raise taxes on the rich and cut your taxes,"* and the votes just pour in. But what the poor don't realize is that historically, liberals don't raise taxes on the rich and the IRS Data proves it.

However, you can't blame the poor for not knowing any better. That's because a willing media, looking for headlines that will sell more advertising, for more dollars, has parroted that lie so many times that the lie has taken on an aura of truth.

When you think about it, it's actually quite easy to understand why the media is so willing to propagate this lie, when they know better.

Understanding the Media

Before going into who really pays taxes, it's very important that you understand how the media selects what you read and hear about any issues of the day and why they select the news stories that you do hear. Please bear with me. I'm going to spend some time on this, because it's important that you understand that what you've heard from the media, concerning taxes (or any other issue, for that matter) may not have painted an accurate picture of the situation.

You see, contrary to popular belief, the news media is not in the business of reporting the truth. They're in the business of **selling "advertising."**

In fact, when you drill down to the most basic business of the so-called news media, they're in the business of making money for their investors and that means selling the most advertising at the highest possible price per column inch or per broadcast second.

It costs a lot more to print that newspaper than the buck or two that you pay for it. The cable news channel that many think of as free, only appears to be free because advertisers pay the bill. Whether it's television, radio, print or Internet, those so-called "news" organizations are first and foremost, in the business of selling advertising, so as to make the most profit possible, for their investors.

It therefore behooves these "news" organizations to have the most attention-grabbing headlines possible. If the media can stir up controversy where there is none, then more people will read or listen to their coverage of that controversy. Their distribution or ratings go up and they can charge more for their advertising. QED.

Man Bites Dog

British newspaper magnate, Alfred Harmsworth, famously summed up this truism, saying, "When a dog bites a man, that is not news, because it happens so often. But if a man bites a dog, that is news."

However, not every news story falls neatly into one of those categories. It then becomes, a matter of which story best fits the Man Bites Dog scenario and will thus help generate the most ad revenue.

Every story that you see on television, hear on the radio, or read in the newspaper or online, has to pass the Man Bites Dog test.

So place yourself in the position of a news desk editor and ask yourself which story is going to sell more newspapers or get more viewers or listeners:

Congressional Budget Office Says Tax Cuts Will Help Poor and Middle Income Earners

- or -

Congressman Windbag Says That Coming Tax Cuts Benefit the Rich

For most tax cuts in modern history, both of the above statements would be true. Here's why.

1) Regardless of the party in power, most tax cuts in the past have primarily benefitted poor and middle income taxpayers more than the rich and

2) There is almost always some congressman, who can be counted upon to "claim" that the tax cuts are "tax cuts for the rich".

This gives the media the opportunity to choose which truth to report. As long as it doesn't violate their agenda, even conservative news outlets will naturally choose the one that will boost their ratings or readership the most.

Gloom and Doom Sells

Furthermore, even though people might want to hear that the latest tax cuts are going to benefit them, the media knows that Gloom and Doom sells more advertising than Sunshine and Roses.

Think about it. When was the last time you saw rubber-neckers slowing down to stare at a road repair crew that was backing up traffic on the other side of the freeway? But a minor fender-bender will slow traffic down for miles in both directions. It's an accident and everyone wants to see what's going on.

The fact that more than one million commercial flights took off and landed safely at their destination, without incident, over the last month, is relegated to the back page of the paper, if it gets printed at all. By contrast, a single small plane crashing in a field gets front-page coverage.

Bad news just sells more than good news and tax cuts for the rich sells more than tax cuts that help everyone.

It's a Disastrous Combination

You've got "Man Bites Dog" and "Gloom and Doom" both working to determine what story the media goes with.

So looking back at those two headlines, it's easy to understand that they'll almost always cite an unfounded gloom and doom statement by a biased congressman, who probably hasn't even read the legislation. At the same time, they generally ignore the fact that statistical research performed by expert neutral parties, such as the bi-partisan Congressional Budget Office (CBO) and neutral economic think tanks, clearly proves that Congressman Windbag's statements are wrong on every point.

But here's the really sly part. By reporting on what someone "said", rather than reporting on the facts, they can create whatever misconception they want, *without lying...* well at least without *"technically"* lying.

You see if Congressman Windbag really did say what the media is reporting, then they have not *technically* lied. They don't let the technicality that they know that the congressman was either wrong or was lying bother them. It's all about ad revenue.

But what it boils down to is that they simply ignore the fact that most tax cuts over the last 50 years have helped the poor and middle class more than the rich. Instead, they report what a biased congressman or political operative said and turn a "Dog Bites Man" yawner into a "Man Bites Dog" headline.

Relying on Press Releases

It gets worse. The truth is further diminished by the fact that the media, in an effort to cut costs and increase profits, increasingly relies on press releases, over actual investigative reporting. You see, it's cheaper to have an editor sort through a thousand press releases a day, to find a few good headlines from the comfort of his office, than it is to send a dozen reporters out to actually investigate the claims of those press releases.

Quite often, newspapers and electronic media will take a well-written, news-ready press release and run it verbatim. I've had that happen with one of mine.

That's why every organization that depends largely on news stories, ranging from congressional offices, political campaigns and PACs, to corporations and unions, have experts on staff, who specialize in writing publication-ready press releases, with Man Bites Dog headlines.

In the end, it often really does come down to column inches or airtime. The editor knows that he has so many column inches or seconds of airtime for a given story and he picks the headlines and focus that will generate the most controversy, even if that story is misleading.

This is a sad indictment of the media. This is because the data that I'll use to conclusively prove that the rich really do pay far more than their share of taxes, is easily accessible public data that the media should be reporting.

I'll show you exactly where to go to get the source data for yourself, from the IRS website. Moreover, it's the raw IRS Collections Data, before any finance geeks or politicians get their hands on it. When you look at this data, you'll quickly realize that the data is irrefutable and leaves no room for argument.

2. How can you know what's true?

OK. So most of the media and many politicians are telling you that the rich don't pay tax and yet, here's this political columnist telling us that the rich pay far more than their share in taxes.

Who do you believe?

How can you know what's true?

Well here's a hint. It has nothing to do with the *"messenger."*

It doesn't matter whether the messenger is a conservative Internet website, a fair and balanced cable news channel, a liberal cable news channel, an ultra-liberal newspaper, or... me. It's not the messenger that's important.

It's the <u>Source</u>.

In fact, despite spin to the contrary and regardless of your opinion of the news organization, the messenger is **NOT** in the business of reporting news. They call themselves *"<u>news</u> organizations,"* but as we've already learned, their real business is in fact, **selling advertising.**

The important point is that it doesn't matter which messenger delivers the story or how many hands it has been filtered through. If you want to measure the accuracy of any news story, you must look to the source.

In the above case, your opinion of the accuracy of the story shouldn't be based on how much you trust Fox, CNN or the local newspaper. It should be based on how much you trust the original source of the news.

Since the messengers in the media are in the business of selling advertising, if you want to know whom to believe, look at the perceived credibility of the **original sources** of the information, if indeed, such sources are provided in the news story.

If a news story doesn't provide credible sources, then regardless of who the messenger may be, you have reason to doubt the validity of that news item. This is what typically happens with tax-related news. It's all about what someone says and not about facts.

As in this book, when you see something in the newspaper, on the Internet or on TV, that news outlet is not generally the source. Unless they're reporting something that they actually saw, as it happened, which is very rare, they're reporting information from some other source.

Regardless of how trustworthy you believe a news outlet to be, you must always look to the original source of the information.

As mentioned earlier, they don't have to lie to boost ratings or readership. By strategically selecting what **sources** they will use or even **what part of the source** they will use, the effect can be just as misleading as a lie.

If you aren't paying attention to original sources, you can be easily fooled.

I am NOT the Source.

The reason I'm making such an issue about sources is because I want you to understand that, as the messenger, I am not the source, but **my source is impeccable.**

The primary source of the data used in this book is the annually published **IRS Collections Data,** along with very basic and very logical calculations, using that IRS data. I'll draw your attention to correlations in the data that you might otherwise miss and I'll provide some basic calculations that you yourself can do, to make the meaning of that data more clear.

But unlike the spinmeisters, who try to convince you that the rich don't pay tax, I won't ask you to blindly accept anything that I report, without providing my underlying source. You'll find footnotes throughout this book, detailing those sources. I encourage you to look up those sources for yourself.

Furthermore, I won't try to mislead you by providing you with just the few small pieces of the data that might tend to prove my point and quietly withhold more pertinent data, as often happens in the media.

Instead, I'll provide you with links to IRS spreadsheets and PDF reports, containing solid data going back to 1986. This annual data is broken down by income percentile and includes:

Total number of returns filed

Adjusted gross income floor on percentiles
(the minimum amount that you had to make to
be included in that percentile)

Adjusted gross income by percentile
(average income for each percentile)

Total income tax collected from all taxpayers
(the total amount of dollars that the IRS
deposited into the US Treasury from all personal
income tax collections)

Income tax collected by percentile
(the dollars that the IRS deposited into the US
Treasury, broken down by income percentile)

Average tax rate by percentile
(the average percent of income that was paid in
taxes, broken down by percentile)

Share of total income earned by percentile
(the percentage of the total of all income earned
by all taxpayers, that the income for each
percentile represents)

Share of total income tax paid by percentile
(the percentage of the total of all personal
income taxes paid by all taxpayers, that the taxes
paid by each percentile represents)

There's no hiding from the facts and you'll have all the
facts. I invite skeptics to try their best to refute any of
the facts in this book. This is the RAW data.

Also included in this book, is similar, related data from a different report on just the top 400 taxpayers, to show you how much even those uber-wealthy individuals pay in personal income tax. All of this data comes from the IRS.

The facts speak for themselves.

I'm only the messenger.

You can't get much more accurate or reliable data about who pays taxes than the IRS Collections Data. It's actually ideal for our purposes, since this data is already broken down by income percentile.

The IRS Collections Data is not even remotely convoluted or hard to understand. In fact, it's very easy to understand. After all, government employees have to be able to understand it, so it can't be too complicated.

If you can understand your own bank statement, then you should be able to understand this IRS data. That's because it effectively amounts to the deposits part of the IRS bank statement to the US Treasury, with deposits broken down by income percentile of the taxpayers responsible for the money being there.

This data represents the actual taxes paid, after all deductions and exclusions. It even takes into consideration any possible cheating on income taxes, since it's what was actually paid to the IRS, by every income group, after all deductions and exclusions; legal or illegal. It's actual money in the US Treasury.

By contrast, the next time you hear a reporter, politician or commentator suggest that the rich don't pay tax, look for their source. In many cases, they won't name a source and when they do, it almost always turns out to be some politician's unqualified spokesman or comes from some convoluted think-tank report that reads like an Escher drawing (i.e. it's impossible to understand).

If you're near a computer and want to follow that IRS report, while reading this book, then download the latest IRS Collections Data, in Microsoft Excel format, right from the IRS website.

There are links provided to the three relevant IRS files, at the end of the next chapter. When you download those files, note that the domain name is "irs.gov" and not some third party. That tells you that you're getting the raw, unmodified data, from the original source.

RAW Data

Keep in mind that every dollar in these reports represents a dollar in the US Treasury. These are the raw numbers, before they've been massaged in any way. They are not projections, nor estimates. They have not been adjusted, factored, normalized, harmonized, homogenized or had any other accounting trick applied to them. There are no assumptions in these numbers that would add bias.

These are the **RAW** numbers, before the accountants, economists and politicians get their hands on them.

This is what the IRS actually put into the US Treasury, broken down by income percentile of the taxpayers responsible for that money being there.

In the primary spreadsheet, the numbers are displayed in descending income categories, so this tells us which income groups actually paid what portion of the tax that was actually **collected**, after all tax breaks and exemptions were applied.

The data concerning the bottom 50% of income earners comes from a second spreadsheet, in which the numbers are displayed in ascending income categories.

In both cases, it's like looking at the IRS bank statement, to the US Treasury and noting the income levels where all of the deposits originated.

There is a third file that you can download, pertaining specifically to the earnings and taxes of the top-earning 400 taxpayers. In it, you can even see where most of the income of that group originated. The top-earning 400 taxpayers are actually a special case and as such, I will have a whole chapter dedicated to this report. The top-400 report is available for download in PDF format and the URL is provided in Chapter 3.

It all comes down to the fact that you can't get more unbiased than money in the bank, along with information on where each dollar originated.

Furthermore, these IRS spreadsheets detail collections going all the way back to 1986. Each year's collections data is released about 18 months after the close of the tax year. It seems that, unlike private business, it takes the government a long time to figure out how much money they collected.

So as of the publication date of this book, the most recent IRS Collections Data available is for the 2009 tax year. This data provides a complete picture - not just a small window that misrepresents the larger picture. This is the kind of transparency that you won't see from anyone who "claims" that the rich don't pay tax.

When you hear such claims, look at their source, if they even cite one. Most often, they'll show you an individual case or two, of a rich person, who pays little or no tax and then try to paint all rich people as being the same. But that's like saying that since one person with red hair robbed a bank, that all redheads are bank robbers.

At the same time, in true "Dog Bites Man" tradition, you won't hear a word in the media about the thousands of wait staff, who are caught failing to report all of their tips each year, since that doesn't sell advertising.

The point is that individual cases are nothing but straw-man arguments.

What you won't get from those who claim that the rich don't pay tax is over-all dollar and cents **proof,** which is what the IRS data that I use, provides.

As you read the rest of this book, keep in mind that everything of which I speak and all of the calculations are based upon that unadulterated IRS Collections Data, for which I have provided you the location, on the IRS website. With those URLs, you can download and verify that data for yourself and even see the entire picture – not just the portion that I'm discussing.

3. 2009 IRS Collections Data

This chapter contains an abbreviated version of the most current IRS Collections Data, which ends with the 2009 tax year. This data, provided by the IRS Statistics of Income Division, is the majority of what I will be referring to throughout this book. Also included is the 2008 IRS Collections Data for the top 400 taxpayers.

The most current IRS Collections Data covers all IRS collections from 1986 to 2009, broken down by income percentile. However, for our purposes, the information in this chapter covers primarily the 2009 tax year, but it also includes limited data from prior tax years.

The data concerning the top 400 taxpayers comes from a related Acrobat (PDF) document, also provided by the IRS Statistics of Income Division. The top 400 report is typically one tax year older than the generic collections data. Although that report is more granular than the more generic data in the spreadsheets, it still includes the same basic totals that tell the real story.

You'll probably notice that the decimal accuracy on these pages is different for the top 400 than for the general collections data. That's because the top 400 report uses a different decimal accuracy.

As mentioned above, the top 400 report is typically one tax year behind the release of the rest of the data. So I had to make a decision. I could base everything on the 2008 tax year or I could include the 2008 top 400 data along with the 2009 tax year data in the spreadsheets. I chose the latter, since the majority of what we'll be examining will be concerning the overall data and I wanted to have the latest overall data with which to work.

Once again, let me remind you that the complete spreadsheets and the PDF document for the top 400 taxpayers are publicly available (though not easy to find) on the IRS website. That's why I provide the links at the end of this chapter. If you plan to download the spreadsheets and PDF document from the IRS website and have them up on your computer as you read the rest of this book, then you can skip to the end of this chapter for the links, since most of the rest of this chapter is just data tables.

We reproduce here, the 2009 data from those spreadsheets and specific other data that we'll be concerned with, along with specific data from the top 400 PDF report, for those who, for whatever reason, have not downloaded that IRS Collections Data.

If you don't have the files open on your computer, then you will probably find yourself referring back to this chapter, from time to time.

[The data tables begin on the next page.]

Total Number of Returns

All Taxpayers = 137,982,203

Top 400 = 400

Top 1% = 1,379,822

Top 5% = 6,899,110

Top 10% = 13,798,220

Top 25% = 34,495,551

Top 50% = 68,991,102

Bottom 50% = 68,991,101
   (Note: Bottom 50% calculated as remainder of
   137 million total returns)

Adjusted Gross Income (AGI)

All Taxpayers = $7,825,389,000,000

Top 400 = $108,204,000,000

Top 1% = $1,324,572,000,000

Top 5% = $2,482,490,000,000

Top 10% = $3,379,731,000,000

Top 25% = $5,149,871,000,000

Top 50% = $6,770,174,000,000

Bottom 50% = $1,055,215,000,000
   (Note: Bottom 50% calculated as remainder of
   $7.825 trillion total income)

Income Taxes Paid

All Taxpayers = $865,863,000,000

Top 400 = $19,593,000,000

Top 1% = $318,043,000,000

Top 5% = $507,907,000,000

Top 10% = $610,156,000,000

Top 25% = $755,903,000,000

Top 50% = $846,352,000,000

Bottom 50% = $19,511,000,000
    (Note: Bottom 50% calculated as remainder of
    $865 billion total taxes)

Group's Share of Total AGI

All Taxpayers = 100%

Top 400 = 1.31%

Top 1% = 16.9266%

Top 5% = 31.7235%

Top 10% = 43.1893%

Top 25% = 65.8098%

Top 50% = 86.5155%

Bottom 50% = 13.4845%
    (Note: Bottom 50% calculated as remainder of
    100%)

Group's Share of Total Taxes

All Taxpayers = 100%

Top 400 = 1.9%

Top 1% = 36.7313%

Top 5% = 58.659%

Top 10% = 70.468%

Top 25% = 87.3005%

Top 50% = 97.7466%

Bottom 50% = 2.2534%
  (Note: Bottom 50% calculated as remainder of 100%)

Group's Average Tax Rate

All Taxpayers = 11.0648%

Top 400 = 18.11%

Top 1% = 24.0110%

Top 5% = 20.4596%

Top 10% = 18.0534%

Top 25% = 14.6781%

Top 50% = 12.5012%

Bottom 50% = 1.8490%
  (Note: Bottom 50% taken from a separate IRS spreadsheet)

Income Floor for Groups

All Taxpayers = (NA)

Top 400 = $109,736,000

Top 1% = $343,927

Top 5% = $154,643

Top 10% = $112,124

Top 25% = $66,193

Top 50% = $32,396

Bottom 50% = (NA)

Other Collections Data from Prior Years

Tax Year 1989

Top 1% Share of Total Taxes = 25.24%

Top 1% of Taxpayers Share of Income for 1989 thru 2009

1989 = 14.19%	1999 = 19.51%
1990 = 14.00%	2000 = 20.81%
1991 = 12.99%	2001 = 17.53%
1992 = 14.23%	2002 = 16.12%
1993 = 13.79%	2003 = 16.77%
1994 = 13.80%	2004 = 19.00%
1995 = 14.60%	2005 = 21.20%
1996 = 16.04%	2006 = 22.06%
1997 = 17.38%	2007 = 22.83%
1998 = 18.47%	2008 = 20.00%
	2009 = 16.93%

Top 1% of Taxpayers Share of Federal Personal Income Tax for 1993 thru 2009

1989 = 25.24%	1999 = 36.18%
1990 = 25.13%	2000 = 37.42%
1991 = 24.82%	2001 = 33.89%
1992 = 27.54%	2002 = 33.71%
1993 = 29.01%	2003 = 34.27%
1994 = 28.86%	2004 = 36.89%
1995 = 30.26%	2005 = 39.38%
1996 = 32.31%	2006 = 39.89%
1997 = 33.17%	2007 = 40.42%
1998 = 34.75%	2008 = 38.02%
	2009 = 36.73%

Top 400 Taxpayers Share of Income for 1992 thru 2008 (not yet available for other years)

1992 = 0.52%	2000 = 1.09%
1993 = 0.50%	2001 = 0.85%
1994 = 0.47%	2002 = 0.69%
1995 = 0.49%	2003 = 0.85%
1996 = 0.66%	2004 = 1.02%
1997 = 0.75%	2005 = 1.15%
1998 = 0.82%	2006 = 1.31%
1999 = 0.91%	2007 = 1.59%
	2008 = 1.31%

Top 400 Taxpayers Share of Personal Income Tax for 1992 thru 2008 (not yet available for other years)

1992 = 1.04%	2000 = 1.58%
1993 = 1.08%	2001 = 1.35%
1994 = 0.99%	2002 = 1.19%
1995 = 1.03%	2003 = 1.37%
1996 = 1.26%	2004 = 1.51%
1997 = 1.23%	2005 = 1.67%
1998 = 1.23%	2006 = 1.77%
1999 = 1.36%	2007 = 2.05%
	2008 = 1.90%

With the exception of the tax rate for the Bottom 50% of taxpayers and all information about the top 400 taxpayers, all of the above data is taken from IRS data that can be found in a spreadsheet at:

http://www.irs.gov/pub/irs-soi/09in01etr.xls

The tax rate for the Bottom 50% was drawn from IRS data that can be found in a related spreadsheet at:

http://www.irs.gov/pub/irs-soi/09in02etr.xls

The collections data for the top 400 taxpayers was drawn from IRS data that can be found in a PDF report at:

http://www.irs.gov/pub/irs-soi/08intop400.pdf

With exception of the information about the top 400 taxpayers, this book is based on the 2009 tax year overall IRS Collections Data, which was released by the IRS in late 2011. The Top 400 IRS Collections Data was pulled from 2008 IRS data, which was released in mid 2011. The top 400 data for 2009 will not be released for several more months.

If you're reading an older copy of this book and the above spreadsheets are out of date, you should be able to find links to the latest versions of these spreadsheets and the PDF file at:

http://TheRichDontPayTax.com/links/

The links on that page will take you to the latest version of these spreadsheets on the IRS website. We try to update those links each year, as soon as the IRS releases the new spreadsheets. Though there have been exceptions, we're usually able to do this within hours of the appearance of the new IRS data on the IRS website.

Caution!

Here is a word of caution. I've been made aware by some of our website visitors that there are phony IRS spreadsheets being distributed. Apparently, some people who don't want the facts that this data exposes to become common knowledge, are trying to disseminate incorrect information. Those phony spreadsheets are designed to look almost identical to the real IRS spreadsheets, but the numbers are dramatically different.

The phony spreadsheets are distributed via email and on websites that are not affiliated in any way with the US government. The authors obviously hope that you won't notice that their spreadsheets are not real IRS publications.

So whenever you download a spreadsheet that purports to be an official IRS publication, always check the URL bar and make sure that it's coming from the **irs.gov** website. That way, you can be sure that you have the original, unadulterated IRS Collections Data.

If you go to the web page link provided above, you will notice that the IRS Collections Data links provided on that page take you directly to the irs.gov website.

Note: Since this data so dramatically contradicts what you may have heard in the past, I must once again, draw your attention to the impeccable source

*of the data. I don't want to sound like a broken
record. But I can't emphasize this enough.*

*These numbers represent dollars actually collected
by the IRS and deposited in the US Treasury, broken
down by the income percentile of taxpayers. The
data has not been massaged in any way. The
numbers represent the raw collections reported by
the IRS, before the accountants, economists, and
politicians get their hands on them.*

4. The Tax Load Percentage to Income Percentage Ratio

How do you fairly measure the tax load of any income group?

That's a tough question that many have debated. The answer had escaped me, too, until I came upon the **"Tax Load Percentage to Income Percentage Ratio."**

As you'll see in a few moments, you can't just look at the amount of dollars paid in taxes by a particular income group, nor the tax rate of a group, nor the group's share of the total tax load. That's because, depending upon changes in economic conditions, each of those metrics can give an erroneous impression.

Dollars Paid in Taxes?

If we look only at **"dollars paid"** in taxes, by any particular income group, then that can be skewed by market conditions.

For example, we might use dollar totals to say that the rich got a tax break in one year, over the previous year, since they paid less in total dollars. But if there were a deep recession and everyone made less money during the second year, then everyone, *including the rich,* would have paid fewer dollars in tax. Do you see where this is going?

In fact, depending upon the cause of a recession, the highest income earners could be hit harder than any other group and therefore owe much less in taxes, even if the government increased taxes on the rich, in that year.

This means that we can't use "dollars paid" as a *reliable* metric of tax load - the key word, being, *"reliable."*

In some years, fewer dollars paid in taxes may not indicate that an income group got a tax break, but could simply mean that everyone, particularly those in that income group, made less money to be taxed, in the first place. It's not a reliable metric.

Therefore, I had to look elsewhere for a reliable metric.

The Tax Rate?

If we look only at the **"tax rate"** that an income group pays, you can be equally deceived. That's because if there is a deep recession and many taxpayers lose lots of money, then the income floor for each income group, except the bottom group, would drop.

Those in the top income percentiles would probably remain in the same percentiles. The richest would remain the richest and the middle class would remain the middle class. But the wealthy, along with everyone else would be making less money. This would drive taxpayers at every income level, with the sole exception of the extremely wealthy, into progressively lower tax brackets for a year or so.

The reason why the extremely wealthy would not drop into a lower tax bracket is because their income places them far above the next lower tax bracket.

In fact, since this very small group represents so much income, the fact that they would run counter to the rest of the taxpayers in this metric, would tend to throw this metric off even further.

However, whether we consider this bias or not, if everyone is earning less across the board, then everyone would be paying tax at a lower rate, as they would fall into progressively lower tax brackets. That's what a progressive income tax does. The rates rise and fall with income.

So looking only at the "tax rate" for the group could make it appear that the upper income group was getting a break, from one year to the next, when all that happened is that many in the group earned so much less that they fell into a lower tax bracket for the year.

Obviously, this was not a reliable metric either.

Percent of Tax Load Paid?

Perhaps the most deceptive measurement of tax load is the **"percentage of overall tax paid"** by each income group. If you don't stop to really think about it, you could easily assume that if the top 1% of taxpayers paid a lower percentage of the total personal income taxes collected from one year to the next, that they were getting a tax break in the second year. But this isn't so.

Once again, the income of each group comes into play. If the overall income of a group remains the same and their share of the tax load drops, then they are indeed, getting a tax break.

But let's look at how easily you can be deceived by the "share of the total tax load" argument. Take a look at the share of the income tax load paid by the top-earning 1% of taxpayers, in tax years 2000 through 2002.

2000 = 37.42% of the tax load

2001 = 33.89% of the tax load
(a relative drop of 9.4%, as calculated below)

2002 = 33.71% of the tax load
(a relative drop of 0.5%, as calculated below)

To calculate the reduction in tax load, you don't simply take the percentage of tax load paid in the first year and subtract the percentage of tax load paid in the next year. Think about it this way.

If your state imposed a 10% sales tax and then they reduced it to 5%, did you get a 5% cut in sales tax? Of course not. Your sales tax was cut in half, meaning that it was cut by 50%. Half of a 10% tax is 5% tax.

So using the above numbers, you have to take the difference in percentage and divide that number by the larger number, to determine the percentage of tax **savings** or **increase**.

So as you look at those numbers, keep in mind that the percentage reduction in taxes paid for the top 1% of taxpayers for 2001 was 9.4%:

(37.42% - 33.89%) / 37.42% = 9.4%

The percentage of tax reduction for the top 1% of taxpayers for 2002 was 0.5%:

(33.89% - 33.71%) / 33.89% = 0.5%

These numbers will be important in a few moments.

Notice that in both 2001 and 2002, the top 1% of taxpayers paid a smaller percentage of the tax load than in the prior year. Those numbers would therefore lead one to believe that the wealthiest taxpayers got significant tax breaks in 2001 and 2002, when exactly the opposite is true, as I'll show you in a few moments.

Those deceptive numbers are exactly what the tax and spend politicians and the news media use to try to convince us that the Bush tax cuts were tax cuts for the wealthy.

Don't get me wrong. I'm no fan of George W. Bush - quite the opposite, in fact. I'm just using this as an example of how the tax and spend politicians and the news media use data that is not germane to the issue, to try to spin this issue to their own ends.

You see, if you look at income levels for each income group, during those years, you'll find that the upper-income earners were earning a smaller portion of the total income in 2001 and 2002, while the lower and middle income earners were actually earning more of the total income.

The effect was a compression of the income earned and income tax scales, with the rich earning less and therefore paying less in taxes, while lower and middle income taxpayers earned more and thus paid more in taxes.

But what those numbers don't show is that while the rich paid less in taxes in 2001 and 2002, their income fell at an even faster rate in those years, meaning that they paid more of the tax load, **based on income share,** than in each prior year - not less.

Let's look at the income percentages for the top 1%, for the same years:

2000 = 20.81%

2001 = 17.53% (a relative drop of 15.8%)

2002 = 16.12% (a relative drop of 8.0%)

Note that these are percentages of the total of all personal income earned in those tax years.

Using the same calculation method that we used above, you'll see that while the top 1% of taxpayers paid 9.4% less of the tax load, in 2001, than they did in 2000, that same group earned a whopping 15.8% **LESS** of the total income in 2001, than they did in 2000.

(20.81% - 17.53%) / 20.81% = 15.8%

Similarly, while they paid 0.5% less of the tax load in 2002, than in 2001, their income dropped a significant 8.0%, in that same time period.

(17.53% - 16.12%) / 17.53% = 8.0%

So if there were no tax breaks or penalties for the top 1% of taxpayers in those years, then their share of the tax load would have dropped 15.8% in 2001, rather than just the 9.4% that it really did and it would have dropped 8.0% in 2002, instead of the 0.5% that it really dropped.

But other times, it could work the other way around. It could make it appear that taxes for the rich rose, when they actually dropped, as happened every year from 1994 to 2000. During the years when Clinton was President, the media tried to make it appear that Clinton was fighting to keep taxes on the rich high, when just the opposite was happening.

So this means that we have to look elsewhere for a fair way to measure taxes by income percentile.

This leads us to the "Tax Load Percentage to Income Percentage Ratio"

There is a problem with trying to use any of the above data to determine changes in tax load, since we're dealing with an income tax. You see, none of the above data takes into consideration routine changes in economic conditions that result in changes in income among every income group.

In some years, the rich make more and therefore, you would expect them to pay more in taxes. But in other years, the rich make less than in prior years, while the middle class makes more. In those years, you would naturally expect the rich to pay less tax, since they earned less on which to be taxed, while the middle class would be expected to pay more tax than in prior years, since they had earned more income on which to be taxed.

All of this means that we have to look elsewhere for an effective measure of the consistency or inconsistency of tax load and to see who really does pay what amount of the overall tax load.

It was when I noticed the inconsistencies in the most commonly cited data for those years, discussed above, that I realized what data I should be looking for. We can't look at any single piece of data. We have to combine two pieces of data and do a simple calculation.

To determine the true tax load of any income group, we need to look at both that groups **Share of Total Taxes Paid** and the groups **Share of Total Income Earned.** With those two pieces of information, you simply take a ratio of the two.

This method ties the group's percentage of total taxes paid by all taxpayers, to the group's percentage of total income earned by all taxpayers. Of course, it works for every income group – not just the top 1%.

This eliminates the effect of economic fluctuations, as applied to either a single income percentile or to all taxpayers.

Let's examine the logic behind eliminating these effects.

When we eliminate the effect of economic fluctuations, as applied to a single income percentile, it means that we are eliminating the bias that would otherwise occur, if one income group earned more, while another earned less, in the same year. Therefore, if the spread of income becomes larger or smaller, between two income groups, you would expect the spread of the tax load to become similarly larger or smaller.

Let's put this into perspective. If one group of taxpayers earns 10% of all of the income earned in one year and the next year, they earn 11% of all of the income earned, *with no changes in the tax code,* you would naturally expect them to pay 10% more income taxes than in the prior year, since they earned 10% more of the income. I know that some people find this concept confusing.

So think of it this way. Let's say that you make widgets and your profit is 10%. Then the economy changes and you are now making an 11% profit. Did your profits increase by 1%? No. Your take-home increased 10%. That's because that 1% increase represents 10% of the original 10% profit.

So back to our original premise, if a particular group were to earn 10% of all income in one year and 11% of all income in the following year, that's a 10% increase and you would expect that same group to pay 10% more tax in that second year, *if there were no changes in the tax rates.*

But if in that second year, that same group were to continue to earn only 10% of all income, but due to changes in the tax code, they were to end up paying 10% more income tax or 10% less tax, then they took a tax hit or got a tax break, respectively.

You see tax hits or tax breaks are actually relative to earnings. It's that ratio of tax load percentage to percentage of total income that tells us who is really getting tax breaks and who is getting tax hits.

So lets say that one income group were to earn, say 20% of all of the income earned in a given year and that this same group were to pay, say 40% of all taxes collected in that year. That would mean that this particular income group was paying double their share of taxes, based on income.

Actually, that's pretty close to what the IRS Collections Data shows happened in 2008, to the top 1% of taxpayers. They earned 20.0% of the income and paid 38.02% of the taxes collected. In other words, they were paying at 1.9 times their share.

Then, in 2009, that same group earned only 16.93% of the total income and yet paid 36.73% of the taxes collected, meaning that they took a tax hit in 2009. Their Tax Load Percentage to Income Percentage Ratio went from 1.9 times their share, to 2.2 times their share. So even though they paid less of the total tax load in 2009, their earnings dropped even more and the end result was that they took a tax hit.

Regardless of how much more or less one income group earns from one year to the next, if there are tax increases or tax breaks given to a particular group, that ratio will change accordingly, from year to year.

Also, by basing our calculations on the total of all income earned, we eliminate the effect of large-scale economic changes. In good times, every income group earns more and pays more in income tax. In a recession, everyone earns less and therefore pays less in personal income tax. So it's only natural that the rich would pay less personal income tax, during a recession.

As you can see, we've eliminated the effect of routine economic fluctuations, whether affecting one income group or all groups and found an effective and reliable way to determine which income groups benefit or are hurt by changes in the tax code. Now, all that we need is access to reliable data about income load and tax load percentages.

Fortunately, the data that we need to calculate this ratio is available in the IRS Collections Data, at which we've been looking.

Let's look at the Tax Load Percentage to Income Percentage Ratio for 2009 (the last reporting year for that data) and this time, we'll do the calculations.

In 2009, the top 1% of taxpayers paid 36.73% of all US Income Tax actually collected.

But in 2009, the top 1% of taxpayers was responsible for earning only 16.93% of total income.

So here's the ratio for the top 1% of taxpayers (income over $343,927):

$$\frac{36.73\%}{16.93\%} = 2.2 \text{ Times Income Share}$$

That's a very straightforward calculation.

The top 1% of taxpayers paid more than double their share of federal personal income tax, based on income, in 2009.

In upcoming chapters, we'll examine this relationship for other income percentiles, to see which income group pays the greatest part of the tax load and how it has changed over the years.

5. What Do All These Numbers Mean?

To begin with, let's look at just a few of the facts that the IRS Collections Data shows us about the 2009 tax year. We'll get around to what these facts mean in a few moments.

- There were roughly 138 million tax returns filed.

- The IRS collected $866 billion in personal income tax.

- The total of all personal income earned was $7.825 trillion.

- The top-earning one percentile of taxpayers (1.38 million taxpayers) earned $1.325 trillion in combined income.

- The top-earning one percentile of taxpayers (1.38 million taxpayers) accounted for $318 billion in income tax paid.

- Based upon that data, the IRS calculated that the top-earning one percentile of taxpayers (1.38 million taxpayers) earned 16.93% of the $7.8 trillion total income earned.
  ($1.325 trillion / $7.825 trillion - 16.93%).

- Also based upon that data, the IRS calculated that the top-earning one percentile of taxpayers (1.38 million taxpayers) paid more than one third (36.73%) of the $866 billion in total individual

income tax actually collected by the IRS.
($318 billion / $866 billion = 36.73%).

Those FACTS completely shatter the spin of the tax and
spend politicians, who want more of our money to
spend, and the media, who just want splashy headlines.
Each, for their own reasons, tell us that the rich don't
pay tax, but they have absolutely **no support** for such
assertions, other than a few isolated cases.

Unlike the spin of those who attempt to convince us that
the rich don't pay tax, this isn't based on a few isolated
cases that are used to paint entire groups with the same
broad brush. This is real money in the US Treasury,
identified by the income percentile of *whole groups,*
who are responsible for that money being there.

As pointed out earlier, since this data represents what
was actually collected by the IRS, it even takes into
effect any under-reporting or "illegal" scams that some
in any group may have got away with. It's what was
actually **"COLLECTED,"** in the end.

Burn that word into your mind. It's **"collected"** dollars
in the US Treasury.

> *Please note that in talking about under-reporting
> or illegal scams, I'm not trying to suggest that the
> rich are alone in evading taxes. In fact, other IRS
> data clearly demonstrates that tax evasion is
> evident in all income groups and is actually more
> likely in several lower income groups.*
>
> *One income group in particular, is far more likely
> to participate in tax evasion than the rich. The
> lowest 20 percentile of taxpayers, which is made*

up largely of wait staff and other service workers, is notorious for under-reporting tips.

We just don't hear about numerous waiters having to pay an extra $500 in taxes and fines, for under-reporting their tips (which could amount to a significant portion of that person's income tax for the year). But the media blasts accounts across the airwaves and newspapers, about a single billionaire having to pay an additional $10,000 in taxes and fines, (which could amount to as little as 1% of his annual tax bill), simply because the IRS chose to "interpret" the tax code differently than his accountants.

Incidentally, we also don't hear about it when a jury of 12 citizens exonerates one of those billionaires. It's not "Man Bites Dog."

So what about the poor?

Let's look at the other end of the scale - the bottom 50% of income earners. They earned 13.48% of the income in 2009, but paid only 2.25% of the taxes actually collected. That's just one-sixth (16.7%) of their share, based on income.

<u>That's a tax break of over 80%!</u>

But before you think that I'm unfairly ragging on the poor, let me say that I understand that the percentage of income that the poor spend in cost of living expenses is higher than the percentage of income that the rich and middle class spend on cost of living expenses. I realize that this would tend to justify lower taxes for poor taxpayers. That's a given.

But stop and think about it for a moment. When we talk about the bottom 50% of taxpayers, we're still talking about people who are in the top economic half of all Americans. That may sound like a contradiction. But it isn't. It's really true.

It has been widely reported by the Wall Street Journal[1], CNN and other news agencies that 47% of Americans pay no US income tax at all. In fact, some even have money "rebated" to them that they never paid in taxes.

The point here is that the desperately poor are not part of the bottom half of taxpayers. They are part of the half of Americans who **PAY NO PERSONAL INCOME TAX AT ALL.**

For our purposes, I'm talking only about those lower income Americans, who are earning enough that, even after all of their tax credits and deductions (child care, dependents, retirement plans, etc.) have been accounted for, still earn enough money to owe some amount of personal income tax.

Those people may be low income, but if they make enough to have taxable income, then that places them

---

[1] Remember to check the sources. Note that neither the Wall Street Journal nor CNN is the source of this report. They reported that the source was the non-partisan, Tax Policy Center (TPC). The TPC reported that they based their calculations on past IRS data, Census Bureau data and recent changes in the tax code. Also the TPC data was vetted by dozens of conservative and liberal media outlets. Then consider that the TPC numbers are in the same range as other similar recent studies. But in the end, you must decide if you trust the source.

among the top economic half (53%) of all Americans.

Since this is so very important, let me rephrase that. If a person earns enough to owe **any** US income tax, then that person is probably doing better than roughly half of all Americans.

If someone is in the top economic half of all people in the United States (the richest nation in the world), then is it fair to call that person poor? After all, he has a job and pays taxes.

The reason I'm making such a point of this is because I'm just trying to put this all into perspective and eliminate the spin. The spin is that the bottom half of taxpayers are poor. The fact is that the bottom half of taxpayers are still doing better than half of all Americans and would be considered rich in most other countries.

So with that in mind, ask yourself, *"Is it fair to tax the rich at more than double their share, based on income, while only taxing the bottom half of 'taxpaying' Americans at one-sixth of their share?"*

I don't begrudge lower income taxpayers a tax break. They should have a tax break. It's only reasonable.

But more than 80%?!!!

What's wrong with this picture? An 80% tax break just seems a little much, for people who are still among the top economic half of all Americans.

Actually, corporate income taxes that are embedded in the price of every retail product that we buy does reduce that disparity, somewhat. In reality, the bottom half of taxpayers are not getting that large a tax break. It's probably rather fair.

But the point that I'm making is that the disparity between the top and bottom income brackets seems unreasonably wide. Many of the top income earners, who are already paying more than double their share, based on income, see that disparity as punishment for a lifetime of hard work and having achieved success.

Don't fall for the isolated case argument.

As I pointed out above, the politicians and the media try to use isolated cases to convince us that the rich, as a whole, cheat on their taxes. They'll trot out the rare case of someone like Leona Helmsley and try to paint all wealthy taxpayers as tax cheats by saying, *"See. We told you that the rich cheat on their taxes."*

Well here's a news flash. It happens that some of the rich do cheat on their taxes. But that's not the whole picture. In fact, there are tax cheats at every income level.

Remember that those most likely to cheat on income taxes are wait staff, who tend to fall into the bottom 20% of income earners and who are notorious for under-reporting tips.

But the media won't mention that the wealthy, as a group, tend to be much more meticulous in filing their taxes than other groups. There is no factual evidence that tells us why this is so. But it might just be that the wealthy have more to lose than most people and don't want to take such a huge risk.

The wealthy also know that their wealth and the complexity of their tax returns makes them the primary targets of the IRS. That's because it's the IRS that gets to decide which conflicting part of the tax code they will enforce. You see, in a complex tax return, there's a better chance of finding some point of conflict, than in a simple one. The wealthy also know that, for the most part, you can't fight the IRS and win and even when you do, the legal fees can be prohibitive.

With the risks so great and the rewards so few, it's not surprising that the wealthy tend to be quite meticulous in filling out their taxes. Sure, there are the few individual cases of tax cheats among the wealthy. But in general, they're like anyone else. They just want to stay on the good side of the IRS and they try their best to obey the law.

Of course, if someone accurately points this out to the media or the tax and spend politicians, he won't get an answer. That's because, when faced with facts that they can't spin, they typically just change the subject.

As soon as they realize that they can't play the cheating card, then they'll trot our some billionaire, like Warren Buffet, and say, *"See. Even when they don't cheat on their taxes, the rich don't pay enough tax."* But that's just another isolated case argument.

In fact, the IRS Collections Data shows conclusively that even the top 400 taxpayers (around one billion dollars or more in net worth) pay far more tax than their share, based on income. They just don't pay as much as the top 1% or top 5% of income earners.

As you'll see later, the only people who should have even the slightest concern about what the uber-rich pay in income tax are those in the top 10% of income earners, but who are not among top 400 taxpayers.

The Whole Picture

The real point here is that we should disregard the spin that the politicians and the media put on who pays what amount of taxes. Instead, step back and take a look at the whole picture, painted by the actual IRS Collections Data and it becomes very clear that the rich (even the top 400) pay far more than their share, based on income and that if anyone is getting a free ride, it's **not** the rich.

Isolated cases make for great headlines and video clips of some tax cheat being led off in handcuffs. But if these cases were representative of high-income earners as a whole, then newspapers, the Internet, and broadcast news would be rife with stories of rich people being led off in handcuffs. That's not happening.

Warren Buffett talks about paying tax at a lower rate than his secretary. But what he doesn't mention is that she's pretty well fixed herself. She isn't a poor girl from the steno pool. In fact, as you'll see in the chapter on the top 400 taxpayers, she and her husband are almost certainly in the top 10% of income earners and this puts them squarely in that small group that does pay income tax at a higher rate than the top 400.

But if you're not in the top 10% of income earners, then you shouldn't be paying tax at a higher rate than Buffett. In fact, if you're not in the top 10% of taxpayers and you are paying income tax at a higher rate than Buffett, then you might want to consider looking for a new accountant or better tax software.

Actually, not all people who are in the upper income percentiles earn their money in the same way as Buffett and the other top 400 taxpayers. While investors like Buffett earn a large portion of their income from investment proceeds and capital gains, most wealthy people actually earn their money from a real business, selling products or services, at a profit.

The reason why many of the top 400 taxpayers pay at a somewhat lower rate is two-fold. To begin with, most of their investment money has already been taxed. But the primary reason is that the IRS wants to encourage long-term investment, which benefits the economy. So the IRS taxes capital gains at a lower rate, in order to make such investments more enticing.

Someone who owns a chain of restaurants across town, for example, can't write off most of his income to capital gains. He may make a million dollars a year. But it's mostly "earned income."

So regardless of whether you're talking about tax cheats or those whose income source allows them to pay at a lower tax rate than some others, the IRS Collections Data shows conclusively that those people are indeed, the exception to the rule.

But so far, we've only talked about the top 1% of taxpayers and the top 400 taxpayers and only in the 2009 tax year. Let's look further.

6.   It's Getting Worse

Here's what's even more surprising.

The IRS Collections Data shows us that the percentage of the tax load that the wealthy pay has been getting steadily worse for high income earners, since the late 80's.

Let's look back at the IRS Collections Data, to 1989, which was the last year that President Reagan could have affected the tax rates. In that tax year, the top 1% of income earners paid 25.24% of all US personal income tax collected by the IRS. That was still far more than their share. But then look forward to the 2009 data and you'll see that the top 1% paid 36.73% of the taxes collected.

That's an almost 50% increase for the top 1% of income earners, since President Reagan left office.

> 36.73% / 25.24% = 1.46
>
> Convert the fraction to percent:
> 1.46 x 100 = 146%
>
> Subtract out 100% to get the increase:
> 146% - 100% = **46% Increase**

It's really not as bad as it sounds. But when I noticed that increase, it got me to looking at other things and I discovered something very surprising.

In general, it's <u>not</u> Democrats who make it worse on upper income taxpayers. It's the Republicans! It was the same people who both the liberal politicians and the media, claimed gave *"tax cuts to the rich!"*

In fact, under the Clinton Administration was when the rich paid less of the tax load, based on income. The top income earners benefitted most during the Clinton years and the IRS Collections Data proves it, beyond any shadow of a doubt.

The following data is the calculated Tax Load Percentage to Income Percentage Ratio (that you've already learned about) for each of those years. See for yourself which party's tax policy benefitted the top income earners most and which party didn't.

Here's the Tax to Income Ratio for the top-earning 1% of taxpayers, from 1993 to 2008.

> 1993 = 2.10 times their share, based on income
> (The first year Clinton could have affected taxes)

> 1994 = 2.09 times their share, based on income
> (The tax share of the wealthy is going down.)

> 1995 = 2.07 times their share, based on income
> (It's still going down.)

> 1996 = 2.01 times their share, based on income
> (Down even more – this is under a Democrat)

> 1997 = 1.91 times their share, based on income
> (And it keeps going down.)

1998 = 1.88 times their share, based on income
(Another good year for the wealthy.)

1999 = 1.85 times their share, based on income
(This is a Democrat reducing taxes on the
wealthiest Americans.)

2000 = 1.80 times their share, based on income
(Who's the friend of the rich? After eight years,
it's clear that it's Bill Clinton.)

2001 = 1.93 times their share, based on income
(The wealthy pay a larger share of taxes, the first
year Bush could have affected taxes.)

2002 = 2.09 times their share, based on income
(The wealthy are paying almost as much of the
tax load as Clinton inherited.)

2003 = 2.04 times their share, based on income
(It starts back down, but remains higher than any
of the last 5 years under Clinton.)

2004 = 1.94 times their share, based on income
(Going down more, but still higher than the last
four years under Clinton.)

2005 = 1.86 times their share, based on income
(Another drop. Maybe Bush is really going to be
a friend to the wealthy.)

2006 = 1.81 times their share, based on income
(It's finally getting down to close to what Bush
inherited.)

$2007 = 1.77$ times their share, based on income
(Seven years into the Bush Administration, the top 1% finally pay a smaller share of the tax load than they did under Clinton.)

$2008 = 1.90$ times their share, based on income
(It was too good to be true. The tax load share of the top 1% goes back up, before Bush leaves office.)

Notice how the Tax to Income Ratio for the top-earning 1% of taxpayers dropped steadily, during the Clinton years, starting off at 2.1 times their share and falling to 1.8 times their share. That means that the share of the income tax burden carried by the rich dropped 14%, under Clinton - a Democrat.

Do the math for yourself:

2.10 times their share inherited by Clinton
-1.80 times their share passed on by Clinton
0.29 difference

$0.29 / 2.10 = 0.138$ fractional decrease

Multiply by 100 to convert to percentage.
$0.138 \times 100 = \textbf{13.8\% \underline{decrease} in tax load}$

But Bush - a Republican - allowed taxes on the rich to bounce right back up to 1.93 times their share, in his first year in office. When the Bush tax cuts took effect in 2002, the top-earning 1% of taxpayers saw their share of the tax load, relative to income share, rise again, to 2.09 times their share that year. Remember that according to the media, these were supposed to be *"tax cuts for the <u>rich</u>."*

Now to be fair, the Tax to Income ratio of the top 1% did trend downward for a few years after that. But in only one of those years (2007) did that ratio fall as low as the tax rate that Bush inherited, but it jumped right back up the next year.

When Bush left office, the Tax to Income Ratio for the top-earning 1% had risen to a level 5.6% higher than the ratio that he had inherited from Clinton.

Do the math for yourself:

> 1.9 times their share passed on by Bush
> -1.8 times their share inherited by Bush
> 0.1 difference
>
> 0.1 / 1.8 = 0.056 fractional increase
>
> Multiply by 100 to convert to percentage.
> 0.056 x 100 = **5.6% <u>increase</u> in tax load**

So, to summarize all of this, the Tax to Income Ratio dropped by 14% for top income earners after eight years, under Clinton, but rose by almost 6% after eight years, under Bush. So which party favors the poor and middle income earners and which favors the rich?

In fact, the Bush tax cuts, far from being tax cuts for the rich, amounted to a tax increase for the rich. The primary beneficiaries of the Bush tax cuts were actually middle-income earners.

So why have we been led to believe the opposite?

Let's face it. As mentioned earlier, the so-called *"news"* media is in the business of selling advertising - not accurately reporting the news. Headlines announcing that the rich are paying more and more taxes don't attract readers or viewers and therefore, such headlines don't increase distribution or listenership and doesn't boost advertising revenue.

The media is now so focused on selling as much advertising as possible, at the highest rates possible, that they have put accurate and unbiased reporting of the news on the back burner.

The result is that for weeks, we heard all the spin about how the Bush tax cuts would be *"tax cuts for the rich."* The media reported only what the left-wing politicians were *saying* and conveniently ignored conservative politicians, the more credible CBO and indeed, any *facts* that would have negatively impacted their circulation or listenership.

Those people and organizations, whose business it is to analyze such bills, correctly predicted that the Bush tax cuts would benefit middle income earners and that if the wealthy were affected at all, they would see a slight increase in taxes. But the media didn't report that.

Furthermore, when the actual data emerged about 18 months after the close of the 2002 tax year, proving that the rich were paying a larger share of the tax load based on income and that middle income earners were the primary beneficiaries of the Bush tax cuts, that revelation was quietly swept under the proverbial carpet.

Not only was it news that wouldn't increase circulation or listenership and therefore lead to increased ad revenue, but it might actually help to decrease ad revenues. So the decision was made to focus on less important issues that would help circulation or listenership and lead to increased ad revenue.

Besides, the legacy media would never admit that they had made a mistake.

The media reports what generates the greatest number of readers or listeners, so as to justify selling their advertising space or seconds for the most money. If reporting unfounded "allegations" by some politician will help increase ad revenue more than reporting numbers from the CBO, then guess what the headline will be.

Note:
Those trying to spin the numbers might argue that even the tax load percentage to income percentage dropped from 2002 to 2007, for the wealthiest 1% of taxpayers. But if they do, they will certainly fail to mention that this ratio went up dramatically in the first two years of the Bush Administration, as a result of the "Bush Tax Cuts", that incidentally, were supposed to be tax cuts for the rich. Critics will also fail to mention that the wealthy ended the Bush years paying more of the tax load, based on income than they did in any of the last four years that Clinton was in office.

7.   Earn more - Pay more and more

It's not just the top income earners, who are paying
more taxes. In fact, The IRS Collections Data shows
that as you move up the income scale, the more punitive
taxes become. In fact, even those in the top 50% of
income-earners are seen as being too successful, in the
government's eyes. Note that in 2009, the income floor,
to be in the top 50% of income earners, was only
$32,396.

So while those in the top 1% of income earners are
paying taxes at a level 2.2 times their share, based on
income, they aren't the only ones being punished for
their success. It's just that as you move down the scale,
the punishment for success drops slightly.

Up to now, we've only been talking about the top 1% of
taxpayers. What about the top 5% or the top 10% of
taxpayers? Let's look down the scale a little and see
what we find.

Here's the Tax Load Share to Income Share Ratio for
the top 5% of taxpayers, in 2009 (those with income
over $154,643):

$$\frac{58.66\%}{31.72\%} = 1.85 \text{ Times Income Share}$$

Here's the ratio for the top 10% of taxpayers, in 2009 (those with income over $112,124):

$$\frac{70.47\%}{43.19\%} = 1.63 \text{ Times Income Share}$$

Is a picture beginning to develop here?

Think about it. When we're talking about the top 10% of taxpayers, we aren't talking about millionaires. We're not even getting close to them. We're talking about people who make as little as $112,124 per year. I mean, think about it...

Lots of IT directors make more than that. Lots of new car salesmen make more than that. Bus drivers in several east-coast cities make more than that. In fact, vast numbers of mid-level government functionaries make more than that.

As you can plainly see, the amount of taxes paid, based on income earned, rises disproportionately, as income rises.

So the next time you hear some politician or someone in the media say that the rich don't pay tax or that the rich are getting a tax break, think back to the IRS Collections Data. Remember that you did the math, on the Tax to Income Ratio calculations for yourself.

Those who claim that the rich don't pay tax have no evidence to support their claim, other than a few rare instances of individuals who make their living on interest only or who cheat on their taxes.

But for every Warren Buffet, who pays a somewhat lower tax rate for a large income, there are tens of thousands of business owners, for whom capital gains and interest income is only a small part of their income and who pay income tax at a somewhat higher rate. For every Leona Helmsley, there are tens of thousands of wealthy taxpayers who don't want to risk the ire of the IRS, by cheating on their taxes.

In fact, the IRS Collections Data shows that the average tax rate for the top 1% of taxpayers, in 2009, was 24.01%, while the average tax rate for the top 50% of taxpayers was 12.5%. Compare that to the average tax rate for the bottom 50% of taxpayers, which was 1.85%.

If the few examples that the tax and spend crowd use to try and convince us that the rich don't pay tax were really representative of the wealthy as a whole, then the IRS Collections Data would show that the rich paid tax at a far lower tax rate and paid far less of the tax load. But it doesn't. As you have seen from the IRS data and in your calculations, the rich pay tax at a much higher rate and pay more of the tax load.

What about tax rates over the years?

Since I point out how the tax and spend crowd like to use rare straw man examples to build a phony case, I feel that I must point out that these numbers are not from just one isolated tax year. In fact, since 1986, which is the first year reported on the IRS spreadsheet, the lowest average tax rate that the top 1% of taxpayers have paid is 22.8%, while during that same period, the highest average rate that the top half of taxpayers paid, was 16.86%.

Of course, the bottom 50% faired even better. During that time period, the highest average percentage tax rate that they paid was only 5.63%.

In other words, the highest tax rates that poor and middle income earners paid in any tax year, since 1986, were far lower than the lowest tax rates paid in any tax year by the top 1% of taxpayers, during that same time period.

But what about "Tax Load Percentage to Income Percentage Ratio," over the years?

To help further insure that I'm not trying to use just part of the IRS data to spin the results, I would also like to point out that the same kind of relationship exists in the ratio of percent of the tax load earned, to percent of total taxes paid, by each income group, over the years.

Remember that to calculate the "Tax Load Percentage to Income Percentage Ratio," you divide the percentage of total taxes paid by the percentage of total income earned. If the result is more than 1, then it means that the group paid more than their share, based on income and if the result is less than 1, it means that the group paid less than their share. Subtract 1 from the number and multiply by 100 to get the percentage over or under their share of income, paid in personal income taxes.

Since 1986, the lowest average ratio of tax load paid in any year, by the **top 1%** of taxpayers, was 1.77 times their share (77% more than their share in 2007), based on income earned. During that same time period, the highest average ratio of tax load borne by the **top half** of taxpayers in any tax year was only 1.13 times their share (13% more than their share in 2009), based on income earned. Then if we look at the ratio of tax load share paid by the **bottom half** of taxpayers, over that same time period, we find that the highest ratio of tax load that this group paid was 0.39 times their share (61% less than their share in 1989), based on income earned.

So even when unfairly commingling data from different tax years, we still can't manipulate the data to even remotely suggest that the rich aren't paying far more of the tax load and much higher tax rates than less prosperous taxpayers.

Do the math yourself.

Remember that this is raw IRS collections data. Look at the numbers and do the math for yourself. Don't depend on the media to do the math for you. Don't depend on me to do it for you. And certainly, don't depend on politicians to do it for you. Their math skills are already suspect, anyway.

In fact, I encourage you to try your best to find a way to twist the IRS Collections Data to even remotely suggest that the rich are even slightly favored by our current tax code or have been at any time in the recent past. You can't.

It's undeniable. At no time since 1986 (the first year of this collections data), have the rich not paid a much higher tax rate and far more of the tax load than less prosperous taxpayers.

If someone tries to tell you otherwise, show him or her the IRS numbers. Ask them to do the math for themselves. Ask them to try to twist the numbers to show anything different. When they do the math for themselves, it's a much more powerful influence than just showing them.

If the media tries to tell you that the rich don't pay tax, then send them the link to the IRS data and show them your calculations. Then challenge them to prove your calculations wrong.

I know of two media outlets that used to rant about the rich not paying tax, which ceased their rants, shortly after receiving a few emails from others, and me, demonstrating how easy it was to disprove their statements on this subject. Granted, neither of them have changed their tune. But they've stopped their rants. They now only resort to insinuations.

I can't take credit for this change. But if those emails didn't have anything to do with it, then the timing was very coincidental. I can only imagine that they realized how easy it is to prove them wrong on this point and they didn't want to be caught lying about something that was so easily disproven.

Part 2:

A Serious Threat to

Our Economy

8.   Why should we be concerned?

Why should ordinary, middle income folks be concerned with a few wealthy people, who have more money than they can possibly spend anyway, having to pay far more than their share of taxes, to support those who pay far less than their share? After all, those rich people can afford to pay a few extra dollars in taxes.

Well the answer is really quite simple, though not necessarily obvious.

Before we go into what's happening nationally, let's take a quick look at what has happened in California over the past few years.

In recent years, California has gone tax crazy, applying the old socialist adage, *"If it moves, tax it. If it keeps moving, regulate it. If it stops moving, subsidize it."* But it's worse than that.

The California tax structure has been heavily discriminating against those with any degree of wealth, both individual and corporate. The result of this *"Soak the Rich"* approach has been a mass exodus of wealth from that state. Most, but not all of this exodus has been to other states, though some of it has actually moved offshore (we'll get to that in a moment).

This exodus of wealth from California is actually endemic of any jurisdiction where successful people feel that they are being punished for their success. The wealthy will take a lot of punishment. But there's a limit to what even the wealthy will take, before they decide to just not take it any more.

Every person, rich or poor, has his own *"economic pain threshold."* Everyone responds differently when that economic pain threshold is breached. Young people may try to borrow money from parents. Others will try to find a better paying job or take a second job. Yet others will go back to school. A few may even turn to crime.

But the point is that when any individual reaches his own economic pain threshold, he takes action to alleviate the pain. The problem that this creates for the ordinary person is in how the wealthy respond to these attacks on success.

You see, although there are many ways to respond to any attack, they all boil down to only three ways. Those three choices are:

Fight, Flight, or Surrender.

Every possible response to every type of attack boils down to one of those three options.

Fight - You can stand and fight. But since, in this case, the government makes the rules, the chances that you'll be able to win are very small. After all, the government does tend to change the rules as they go. The wealthy know this and they didn't make all their money by making bad decisions or initiating battles that they were likely to lose.

Surrender - You can surrender. But we're talking about people who have been successful and that means that we're talking about people for whom the word, *"surrender"*, is not even part of their vocabulary.

That leaves **Flight.**

The wealthy, the successful and the driven people are leaving California and heading to states like Texas and Florida, in order to preserve what's left of what they have built.

You see, when the economic pain is coming from government, there is only one way to relieve that pain. It means moving to a jurisdiction where there is less or even no economic pain.

The problem for ordinary, non-wealthy Americans is that those wealthy taxpayers, who are looking for a place to protect what they have built, are now discovering that even moving to another jurisdiction within the USA only provides partial and likely temporary relief. After all, the US government is now adopting California's *"Soak the Rich"* mentality and there is no place within the USA where one can escape those federal attacks.

You see, unlike California's punitive attacks on success, federal attacks on success reach across all state boundaries. As more and more large taxpayers are discovering, finding relief from federal attacks on success, often means moving to another country and taking all of your assets with you.

Think of it this way. If a child touches a lit match, he soon learns to avoid touching lit matches. Similarly, if a wealthy person is punished beyond his economic pain threshold, for the supposed crime of being successful in the USA, he soon learns that the only way to avoid that pain is to avoid the USA, which means investing outside the USA.

But in the case of the USA, we have what is termed a "non-territorial tax system". That means that US citizens and permanent residents are taxed on their worldwide income, regardless of where that income is derived, banked or spent. So if the wealthy are to move their investments elsewhere and expect to avoid punitive US taxes, the only way that they can do that is to leave the USA and take another citizenship.

Some renounce their US citizenship upon acquiring a new one. But many more adopt the posture of *"escape."* Many expats refer to this as *"not telling the jailer where you're going."* Due to a number of recent laws meant to punish expatriation of the wealthy, including a punitive, first ever, US Exit Tax[2], signed into law by George W. Bush, many expats now simply drop off the US radar.

By the way, many US expats refer to this Exit Tax as the "Reichsfluchtsteuer"; a reference to the "Jew Taxes" imposed by Hitler, in 1931, to keep wealthy Jews from leaving Germany with their wealth intact.

Those who drop out, move offshore, get a new passport (or two), start paying taxes in their new country and stop paying US taxes. Sure, this means that they can

---

[2] The Heroes Earnings Assistance and Relief Tax Act (HEART), contains the first ever US Exit Tax.
http://thomas.loc.gov/cgi-bin/query/z?c110:H.R.6081.ENR:

never return. But many of them take the attitude of, *"Why would I want to return to a country that punished me for being successful, creating jobs and paying far more than my share of taxes?"*

I know that it's hard to imagine an American holding that attitude. But having lived in London for a time (though I maintained my US home), I met many US expats there and that attitude was pervasive.

Permanently leaving the USA may sound like a drastic move. That's certainly what I thought, when I first began investigating this phenomenon. But I've learned that **millions** of Americans are taking that drastic step each and every year.

That's right. It's not just a few people who are leaving. US citizens are leaving the USA in huge and growing numbers. They even have a name for themselves. They call themselves, *"taxpatriates" or "taxpats."*

According to a series of studies commissioned by New Global Initiatives and conducted by Zogby International, Zogby[3], *"by a moderate estimate" (Zogby's words)*, more than three million Americans relocate outside the USA every year. But this raises a serious question:

"How many of those people are poor?"

Let's be reasonable. The poor don't leave the USA.

---

[3] Barrons (September 24, 2007): "The silent U.S. emigration" http://online.barrons.com/article/SB119041441207935747.html (This is an article by the client of the Zogby study, citing some of the results of the study. The "moderate estimate" statement is part of the original Zogby press release, no longer available online.)

They can't afford to leave all of our free benefits. In fact, they come wading across the Rio Grande River, by the hundreds of thousands every year. They crowd our classrooms and our hospital waiting rooms that they don't pay for, thus placing an additional burden on our economy – a burden that falls to you and me to pay for, with *our* taxes.

But it's an entirely different story for the rich. Not only can they easily afford to leave, but they're also the exact same people to whom the government is giving the greatest incentive to leave.

Consider too, that a huge market has developed in recent years, catering to US expats and particularly, to wealthy US expats. Companies like The Sovereign Society[4], International Living[5], Escape Artist[6], and Live and Invest Overseas[7] are just a few that have seen a significant upsurge in business, in recent years. But it's where this business is coming from and the motivation of their clients that tells the story.

I contacted former US Congressman Bob Bauman, JD, who is now the Legal Council for both The Sovereign Society and International Living and asked him about the growth of those businesses. This is just a portion of his response.

"During 2009 and continuing today, the Sovereign Society and International Living, have both

---

[4] The Sovereign Society, http://www.sovereignsociety.com/

[5] International Living, http://internationalliving.com/

[6] Escape Artist, http://www.escapeartist.com/

[7] Live and Invest Overseas, http://www.liveandinvestoverseas.com/

experienced a marked increase in interest among many people who are considering moving assets and themselves offshore.

This is evidenced by unprecedented increases in our membership and much higher attendance at our offshore conferences.

My personal talks with many of these Americans shows a very real fear about the current policies of the US government..."

Rep. Bauman's statement is one of the most telling statements on this subject. Note the key phrases, *"unprecedented increases in membership"*, *"much higher attendance"*, and *"very real fear."*

Keep in mind that while such organizations provide services to a broad economic range of expats and the costs for their services are generally not prohibitive, most of their clients are naturally going to be among the upper income groups, simply because those with the most money, have the most to lose and are therefore more willing to pay for such services.

"So what? Let'em leave!"

When I address this issue in a live presentation, I stop the presentation at this point and ask the attendees what they think of this flight of wealth. I don't try to elicit any particular type of response.

Yet invariably, the vast majority of responses are along the lines of calling those expats names, such as *"traitors"* or *"cowards"* and statements along the lines of, *"Well, so what? Let'em leave! If they don't want to stay in the greatest nation on Earth, then we don't want'em!"*

Remember that I said some of the things in this book might make you angry. Well this is one of them. That was my first response, too. But prepare for a shock.

Such attitudes only show a significant naiveté, concerning the end result of such expatriation of wealth. You see, like them or not, we <u>need</u> those wealthy expats and the investment and tax dollars that they take with them, when they leave. Those investment dollars represent jobs that are going offshore and the tax dollars... well... we'll look at that in a moment.

Like most people, those who are leaving would prefer to be liked. But when all that they have worked for is at risk, they forget about who likes them and who doesn't. We can call them every vile name in the book and it won't affect them in the least. You see, their assets represent more than money to them. They represent years of long hours, hard work and risks.

They don't want the fruits of their labor taken away from them and given to some deadbeat "Occupy" type, who's too lazy to work at all.

In fact, calling the wealthy names only convinces more of them to leave. Just think about it from a different point of view, for a moment.

If you were to tell your co-workers that you were thinking about taking a job with a competing company, but that you had not yet made up your mind, which of the following responses would make you more likely to stay and which would make you more likely to take that other job.

A) All your co-workers tell you how they will miss you, how valuable you are to the company and they all wish you luck, should you ultimately decide to leave, or

B) All your co-workers tell you that if you want to be a traitor to the company, just go ahead and leave and they call you vile names.

Tough question, huh?

Well something along the lines of the above option "B," is what the wealthy, who are only beginning to consider the possibility of leaving, are facing from their friends and neighbors, when they announce that they're *"considering"* the possibility of leaving.

When we berate those who don't want to leave in the first place, but who are being put in an increasingly untenable position, we only help them make up their minds to leave.

On the other hand, if we make them feel wanted, that could very well help to increase their economic pain threshold and convince them to stay and keep fighting the good fight.

What do we have to lose?

Think back to the IRS Collections Data. In 2009, the top 1% of income earners, which amounted to just 1.38 million taxpayers, paid 36.73% of all federal personal income tax collected in that year. Remember too, the *"moderate estimate"* from Zogby, that more than three million Americans relocate outside the USA every year. Also consider that the term, "relocate" was Zogby's term; not mine. When I lived in London I didn't "relocate". I kept a home in the USA. When a person relocates, he moves his home.

To help you visualize the problem, the following pie chart gives you a representation of the issue at hand. The entire pie represents the total of all personal income tax collected.

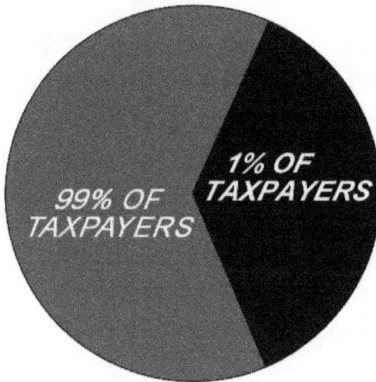

Figure 1: Just 1% of taxpayers pay more than a third of all personal income tax collected.

So ask yourself what you think the government would do if they lost more than a third of the revenue that they were collecting from personal income taxes. Would they cut spending to account for having a third less revenue or would they raise the taxes of those who remain? Think about it...

Now I'm not suggesting that all of those expats are among the top 1% of taxpayers. In fact, I think that it's only reasonable to assume that those expats are spread across a number of upper income categories.

Just keep in mind that those with the most incentive to leave, are those who are being punished the most for their success, regardless of age. Then consider that the further up the income scale a taxpayer is, the more he is punished for his success and the more incentive he has for leaving.

But what's worse is that this same group is comprised of the people who can most easily afford to leave. When the cost of staying in the USA becomes higher than the cost of living elsewhere, the successful will naturally start looking at living elsewhere. QED.

Therefore, it's only fair to conclude that the list of those who are leaving is probably weighted rather heavily toward those US taxpayers with both the most means and most motive. Of course, the people who have both the most means and the most motive for leaving are the wealthiest of Americans.

Certainly, not all of any one income group will leave. Some are physically unable to travel. Others may have business interests here that just wouldn't work in any other country or that would require years to move. Then there are those who may have family ties here, such as non-custodial parents or those who have elderly parents who can't or won't leave. Just remember that the further up the income scale a person is, the more incentive he has for leaving.

But the fact remains that many of the wealthiest Americans are leaving the USA and you have to consider how that will affect you. It's now time to stop thinking about the wealthy and think about how this wave of wealth expatriation will affect **YOU.**

Let's take a look at that pie chart again, but this time, with a different view. Let's look at what happens when the top income earners... leave.

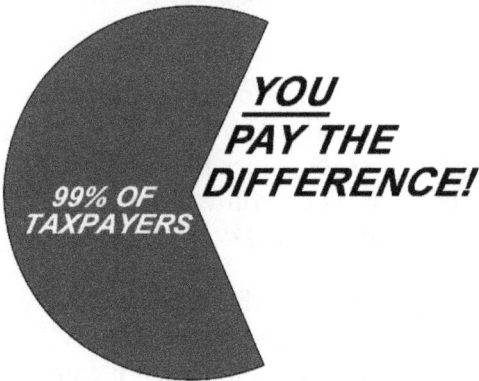

Figure 2: Consider what happens if only the top 1% of taxpayers leave the USA.

Have I got your attention?

If just the top-earning 1% of all US taxpayers were to leave the USA, it would mean that the remaining taxpayers would have to make up the difference, to the tune of an almost 60% tax increase. Do the math.

100% - 36.73% of taxes = 63.27% difference

36.73% / 63.27% = **58% tax increase**

That's not the multiplier. That's the increase beyond 100%. So you take last year's tax bill and add 58%.

Can you afford a 60% tax increase? (Multiply your last year's tax bill by 1.58, for the answer.)

Now while you're thinking about the effect of the top 1% leaving, consider that the top 5% of income earners paid 58.66% of all federal personal income taxes collected, in the same tax year and that the top 10% paid 70.5% of all federal personal income taxes collected.

Let's do the math for those two groups.

Since the top 5% of taxpayers pay 58.66% of all federal personal income taxes collected, here's what it would mean to those who remain, should that group leave.

100% - 58.66% of taxes = 41.34% difference

58.66% / 41.34% = **142% tax increase**

Can you afford to pay almost one and a half times more income tax than you pay now? (Multiply your last year's tax bill by 2.42, for the answer.)

Since the top 10% of taxpayers pay 70.5% of all federal personal income taxes collected, if the top 10% were to leave, here's what it would mean to those who remain.

100% - 70.5% of taxes = 29.5% difference

70.5% / 29.5% = **239% tax increase**

Of course, it will never get that bad, because long before it does, the US government will impose strict border controls. However, those controls will only be on those who want to **leave.** After all, it seems that the government wants to welcome anyone who wants to come here – even without documentation.

But do you begin to see where this could become a serious problem for those of us who stay. As more and more wealthy taxpayers flee to more wealth-friendly jurisdictions, it means that those of us who remain will be taxed more, to make up the difference.

Now I know that not all of any one income group is going to leave. As mentioned earlier, some have too many ties here, to make fleeing the USA an acceptable option. Others keep hoping against the odds, that things will get better and they keep staying a little longer and a little longer. But as more and more of their wealthy friends leave, they begin to look more closely at that option, themselves.

The above calculations are based on all of a particular income group leaving, because that's the only data that we have available. But if you look at those numbers and at how the calculations were made, you can begin to see that whatever the income spread of those who are leaving, it doesn't paint a pretty picture for those of us who stay.

9.   The Underlying Problem

Let's look back at how the tax code has been used - or rather abused - over the years, by both parties, in an effort to try and favor their own big donors. It should be obvious that the problem is not in the myriad **changes** that have been made to the tax code, but rather the **tax code itself**.

Lawmakers of both parties have found our current tax code to be fertile soil for cultivating their own form of favoritism – favoritism that more often than not, benefits their big donors over their individual constituents.

Who benefits from tax breaks?

Congress gives tax breaks to people and companies, based on what those people and companies buy, sell, or build. They give breaks based on the technologies that a company employs or how individuals or companies invest their money. They give tax breaks for all kinds of things – many that make no sense at all.

Today, the tax code is infested with huge numbers of such tax breaks. There are so many tax breaks that major accounting firms now employ legions of specialized accountants, who focus only on narrow groups of tax breaks.

If an individual client has certain types of investments or employs certain business practices, then they bring in one of the experts on that area of the tax code. Other conditions may require a different expert.

I know a gentleman who owns a local business and has both domestic and offshore investments. He's not what most people would call rich, but he's certainly not poor, either. I mention him because last year, he told me that the accounting firm that he uses to fill out his tax return, employs four accountants to calculate his taxes.

We're not talking about a billionaire here, folks!

This is a man who owns a local business, with just one location. But our tax code has become so complex and rife with conflicting rules and regulations and even more conflicting decisions on how those regulations are to be interpreted that not only can he not fill out his own tax forms himself, but no single accountant at his large accounting firm can fill it out properly, without help from specialists.

But these tax breaks are not just for the rich, as a whole. They are most often aimed at helping one group of rich people or corporations to gain an advantage over another group of rich people or corporations. A few years later, control of the government changes and those tax breaks are reversed, to favor a different group of rich people or corporations.

It's because so few rich people and corporations are affected by any group of tax breaks that the rich, **as a whole**, continue to pay so much more of the tax load than their share of income would justify.

Note: According to the previously mentioned IRS data, the top 400 taxpayers, which is about three hundredths of a percent (0.03%) of all taxpayers, tend to pay slightly less than most of the rest of the top 10%, since a larger portion of their income is derived from investments and long-term capital gains. Roughly, those are the 400 US taxpayers who have a net worth of about one billion dollars or more. We'll deal with this in the next chapter.

You see, by and large, most wealthy people and most medium and small sized companies don't have lobbyists in Washington. So even most rich people don't benefit from those tax breaks. Some may find a way to change the way they make money to take advantage of changes in the tax code. But about the time that they adjust their finances to take advantage of the changes that were enacted a year or two earlier, the tax code changes again.

But the worst of all is the tax on corporate income. That's because taxing businesses of any size allows the government to hide vast amounts of taxes from naive citizens. You see this naiveté very clearly, in the demands from uninformed citizens to tax the corporations more. They don't realize that in the end, corporations don't pay tax.

Only people pay tax.

There is a misconception that has been perpetrated by the tax and spend politicians and the media. They want us to believe that corporations pay income tax.

They DON'T!

Corporations don't pay tax. Partnerships don't pay tax. Sole proprietors don't pay tax.

Only people pay tax.

If it doesn't eat, breathe, laugh, cry, and complain about government, then it doesn't pay tax.

There are those who would point out that corporations file and pay corporate income taxes. But what those people fail to understand is that to any company of any size, taxes of every kind are just another *"cost of doing business"* that must be factored into the price of their products or services. Of course, as with other costs of doing business, the business adds something to that cost, as a profit.

If the cost of steel goes up, then automobile manufacturers raise the price of their cars. If the price of grain goes up, then bakers raise the price of bread. And if corporate income taxes go up, every company in the United States raises the prices of all of their products or services.

Companies, be they large corporations, small sole proprietorships or anything in between, don't pay tax. They just factor the cost of those taxes into the price of their products or services and pass those taxes on to the next buyer in the chain, till the final living, breathing consumer ends up paying all those levels of taxes.

Interestingly, this applies not only to income taxes, but to Value Added Taxes (VAT), property taxes, and licensing fees, such as liquor licenses. Regardless of whatever form of tax any branch of government imposes on business, it is the final, living, breathing consumer, who ends up paying all those levels of taxes and fees.

Actually, the consumer ultimately pays for all the levels of compliance costs required to calculate those taxes, as well, along with a bit of profit on that cost. That's because, whatever additional accounting costs a company incurs to handle income tax compliance and filing are also passed on to the final, living, breathing consumer, with a little profit added.

In the end,

Only People Pay Tax.

10. The Top 400 – A Special Case

As mentioned earlier, the top-earning 400 taxpayers are a special case, even among the top 1% of taxpayers. On average, the top 400 do pay a little less in taxes than most others in the top 10% of income earners.

These are people whose net worth probably, but not necessarily, exceeds one billion dollars. Several sources, including Forbes Magazine, seem to agree that, at this point in time, there are around 400 billionaires in the USA[8]. Perhaps that's why the IRS chose that number. But then, it may be that they just picked a number out of the hat. It's the IRS, so who knows.

But in general, I think that it's fairly safe to assume that most, if not all of that top-earning 400 taxpayers have a net worth exceeding one billion dollars and that there are likely not very many more billionaires in the USA, beyond that number.

The reason why these people are a special case is because as a person approaches that billion dollar threshold, he tends to make a larger share of his annual income from dividends and capital gains, which are taxed at a lower level than ordinary income. In fact, as the IRS Top 400 Collections Data shows, that group

---

[8] In 2006, the Forbes List of 400 Wealthiest Americans included, for the first time, only billionaires. In the previous year, there were 374 billionaires on that list. In 2009, the number dropped below 400, to 391 billionaires, but the list once again exceeds 400. Since the list is only 400 names long, we can't know how many more there may be. But it seems to be hovering at around 400. Note too, that the Forbes lists are not definitive. They just provide a reasonable base for discussion.

earns 56.81% of all of their income from capital gains (Col 35 of the Top 400 Report).

Look at all the facts.

Once again, I must warn you to not fall prey to arguments that seem to be too pat, especially when it involves an individual example. Look at all the facts.

For example, a few months ago, Barack Obama trotted out Warren Buffett, in an attempt to prove that the rich don't pay enough tax. Obama had Warren Buffett up there saying that he paid tax at a lower rate than his secretary.

While that is technically true, that statement leaves many misconceptions hanging ominously in the air.

The Rate –

While Buffett, who is one of those top 400 taxpayers, does by his own admission pay tax at around 17.4%[9], that tax rate doesn't tell the whole story. You see, the reason why he pays tax at that rate is two-fold.

First, he paid tax on the money that was used in his long-term investments, when he originally earned it.

But more importantly, the government wants to encourage long-term investments, so they offer a preferred tax rate on capital gains, since that invested

---

[9] Warren E. Buffett (Op-Ed), "Stop Coddling the Super-Rich", New York Times, August 14, 2011, http://www.nytimes.com/2011/08/15/opinion/stop-coddling-the-super-rich.html?_r=1

money is typically tied up for an extended period of time.

In the interest of fairness, every taxpayer, regardless of income level, pays the same capital gains rate. If you sell a rent house and make a lot of money on the sale, you pay the same capital gains rate as Buffett, on the profit from that sale. If you sell the Apple stock that you've been holding since 1980 and make a lot of money on it, you pay the same capital gains rate as Buffett, on the profit from that sale.

The point is that the capital gains rate is lower for a reason and it's the same rate for everyone. But that's not the whole story.

The Hype –

The real problem with the Buffett Spin is that it tries to make it appear that people like Buffett pay less than **"everyone"** else. Note that I emphasized the word "everyone."

You see, if you look at all of the facts, including the IRS Collections Data, you will see that by paying tax at around 17.4%, Buffett's tax rate is about the same as the average for the top 400 taxpayers, which is 18.11%.

But the more important thing that you should notice is that the only income group that pays at a higher tax rate than the top 400, are those in the top 10% of taxpayers, who are not among the top 400. Let's look back at the IRS Collections Data and see what tax rates were paid by each income percentile.

Top 400 = 18.11%

Top 1% = 24.011%

Top 5% = 20.4596%

Top 10% = 18.0534%

Top 25% = 14.6781%

Top 50% = 12.5012%

Bottom 50% = 1.849%

As you can see from the IRS Collections Data, if you're in the bottom 90% of income earners, then it's a pretty safe bet that you pay tax at a lower rate than the top 400 taxpayers.

It follows then that the only people who have any reason to complain about the tax rates paid by the top 400 (including Buffett) are those who are in that top 10%, but who are not among the top 400... and those taxpayers aren't complaining.

More Hype –

Buffett and Obama like to point to Buffett's secretary, as an example of someone who pays income tax at a higher rate than her billionaire boss. But what they don't tell you is that billionaires don't hire some girl fresh out of the steno pool, to be their secretary. They hire the most highly qualified professional secretary available. Such secretaries are usually paid very well.

In fact, although we don't know exactly what Buffett's

secretary earns, the fact that she has spent the last 38 years[10] working for Berkshire Hathaway and the last 19 of those years[11] working directly for one of the wealthiest men in the world, tells us that unless Buffett is a cheap skate, she's probably doing pretty well.

But let's take it a step further. Buffett revealed that his secretary pays tax at the rate of 38.5%. A look at the tax tables and a little basic math should tell you that if she and her husband paid income tax at that rate, their combined income should be somewhere between $200,000 and $500,000 per year.

But even that assumes that if they earned at the low end of that range ($200,000) and paid at the 38.5% rate, they must have very poor tax preparers – something that would not be expected of Buffett's secretary.

If they paid at 38.5%, it would be extremely difficult to have a combined income any less than $200,000. Now look back at the IRS Collections Data. You'll see that to be among the top 5% of income earners, you have to have made at least $154,643, in 2009. To be among the top 1% of income earners, you need to have made at least $343,927. So do the math.

Based on that very straight forward calculation, Buffett's secretary and her husband are certainly in the

---

[10] John Hayward, "The most important paycheck in the world", Human Events, January 26, 2012, http://www.humanevents.com/article.php?id=49075

[11] "Warren Buffett and His Secretary Talk Taxes", ABC News, January 25, 2012, http://abcnews.go.com/blogs/business/2012/01/warren-buffett-and-his-secretary-talk-taxes/

top 5% of US income earners and quite possibly in the top 1% of US income earners.

They're **NOT** poor.

Such a conclusion is supported by the fact that Buffett's secretary and her husband just bought a second home in Surprise, Arizona[12]. The four bedroom, two and a half bath, second home has a pool and a Professional PGA putting green, in the back yard. According to real estate records, they paid $144,000 for that second home.

Sure, $144,000 is not a lot for a home. But how many poor people do you know who can afford to buy a second home of any kind, in another state?

So it seems clear that the reason why Buffett pays tax at a lower rate than his secretary, is because his secretary and her husband fall well into that limited group of the top 10% of income earners, who are not among that top 400 taxpayers.

It's all hype.

The fact is that the only people who pay income tax at a higher rate than those top earning 400 aren't complaining. They're in the top 10% and too busy trying to reach that high income level themselves.

The truth is that at least 90% of taxpayers already pay income tax at a significantly lower rate than Buffett and most of his cronies, so they have no reason to complain.

---

[12] "Despite Unfair Tax Burden, Warren Buffett's Secretary Was Just Able To Buy A Second Home", The Smoking Gun, January 25, 2012, http://www.thesmokinggun.com/buster/warren-buffett-secretary-homes-654812

But let us not forget that half of Americans pay no income tax at all and some even get money rebated that they never paid in tax. Therefore, it turns out that it's not just the bottom 90% of taxpayers that pay income tax at a lower rate than the top 400. It's really the poorest 95% of all Americans.

So it turns out that even the arguments of the tax and spend politicians, regarding the top 400 taxpayers, are like the rest of their *"Soak the Rich"* arguments.

They're all hype.

Part 3:

A Fair Solution

11. Defining The Problem and What Constitutes Success

There are two steps that must be taken before attempting to structure a solution to any problem. The first step is to separate the problem from the symptoms, so as to define the real problem. The second step is to establish what will define a successful solution. Only when you have completed both of these steps, are you ready to tackle the problem.

So before we try to sculpt a solution to the tax situation that we face today, let's define the problem and what constitutes success.

Defining the Problem

The first step in solving any problem is to define the real problem. You have to tear away the façade of symptoms, to get to the source of the problem.

It's only a symptom that people at every income level, high enough to owe any income tax, feel that they are being treated unfairly. It's only a symptom that hundreds of thousands of jobs are being sent offshore, every year. It's only a symptom that the wealthiest and most prolific taxpayers – the producers and innovators – are leaving the USA in record numbers.

It should be obvious by now that the underlying problem is **not**, "who pays tax" or "how much they pay," but rather, at least in large part, the tax system itself. Our current tax system began as a very simple

27 page, low-rate, flat income tax. But the problem with an income tax is that it provides fertile ground for playing favorites and it wasn't long before members of both parties in Congress realized that.

Withholding made it even worse. Since many people don't look at their pay stub and think about how much they're really paying in income taxes, the term, *"Out of sight - out of mind"* applies. Furthermore, as a result of withholding, studies now show that many American taxpayers no longer think of that withheld money as *"their money,"* even though it is.

In the end, although the income tax likely began with good intention, it has ballooned into the most onerous and complex set of regulations in US history. Under this warped system, half of Americans now pay no personal income tax[13], while just one-half percent of Americans pay over a third of all personal income taxes.

Is it any wonder then, why so many upper income taxpayers are fleeing the USA in record numbers? Although there are other issues that are also driving this flight of wealth, it's obvious that our convoluted and often punitive tax system is one of the leading reasons for it.

Of course, it should also be noted here that a heavy progressive income tax was the **second plank of the**

---

[13] Roberton Williams, "Who Pays No Income Tax?", The Tax Policy Center (a joint venture of the Urban Institute and Brookings Institution), July 02, 2009,
http://www.taxpolicycenter.org/UploadedPDF/1001289_who_pays.pdf
Note: The Tax Policy Center is said to be non-partisan, but in the end, you must decide how much trust you place in this source.

Communist Manifesto. Not exactly a resounding endorsement of our current income tax, is it?

The plain fact is that it's not the tax rate or who gets tax breaks that is the problem. Those are just the symptoms of a far worse problem.

The underlying problem is the progressive income tax. That's our starting point.

Defining Success

The second critical step in attacking any problem is to define what constitutes success.

After all, how can you possibly expect to craft a viable solution to any problem, if you don't have any idea what your ultimate goal should be? Just knowing what the problem is, does not automatically imply a particular solution.

If your roof leaks, that's just the problem. But a successful solution to your problem is not simply patching the roof. You want the repair to look good. In other words, you don't want the patch to look like a patch. You want the repair to be long-lasting and not start leaking a month later. And of course you want the cost to be as low as possible, within the confines of a quality job.

The best problem-solvers know that before attempting to develop a solution, you must first define what will constitute a *successful* solution.

One of the major flaws in the way Congress and most Presidents approach solving problems is that they fail to define exactly what will constitute success, before tackling a problem. However, despite what you may think, it's not incompetence that leads them to this flawed approach to problem solving. It's actually planned that way.

You see, by not defining what constitutes success before passing legislation, it allows our elected officials to later look at the results – however inconsequential those results may be – and claim that those results are what they were striving for. Without predefined goals, then regardless of how insignificant the results may seem to you, it allows lawmakers to claim that any result constitutes great success.

Then they tell us that because they were so successful last time, they need to pass more legislation and spend even more of our money, to achieve even more success – but again, without defining what is supposed to constitute that next level of success.

But since I've had to solve problems in the real world, where my business profits or my employer's business profits depended largely upon my solutions being truly successful, I'm not going to play those games with you. I'm going to define what I think should constitute success in tax reform, before going any further. See if you agree with my goals.

In fact, after you read my list of goals, you may even want to add some of your own. But I think that you'll agree that if we achieve even half of the goals on this list, our tax reform will constitute a huge success.

Let me be clear. These goals are not all required in order to claim success. Rather, they are measures of success. How many of these targets can be achieved and to what level, will tell us how successful we've been.

1. **Clear and Simple** – A tax plan should be easy to understand and easy to comply with. It should not require any "expert" in order to insure compliance.

2. **Transparent** – The taxpayer should see every cent that he is paying. No taxes should be hidden.

3. **Fair to ALL** – Every taxpayer should be treated exactly the same. In fact, a truly fair solution should make it difficult for Congress to play favorites.

4. **Un-Intrusive** – One of the major problems with our current tax system is that it gives the government an unwarranted window into our personal finances. This window into our personal finances needs to be removed.

5. **Un-Tax the Cost-of-Living** – Earnings or expenses up to the poverty line should not be taxed (if you're thinking that we should do this only for the poor, see #3).

6. **Increase Compliance** – While there will always be those who will try to cheat on their taxes, an effective solution will increase compliance. The amount of such increased compliance will help us measure our success.

7. **Reduce Compliance Costs** – Every year, Americans pay billions in embedded compliance costs on their retail purchases. Those compliance costs need to be drastically reduced.

8. **Reward Savings and Investment** – Since savings and investment boost the economy, savings and investment should not be taxed.

9. **Tax the Underground Economy** – Any solution should capture as much tax as possible from the underground economy – drug dealers, bookies, illegal aliens, etc.

10. **Repatriate Off-Shored Jobs** – Any solution should create incentives for companies that have moved jobs offshore, as a way of reducing taxes, to bring those jobs back to the USA.

11. **Repatriate Lost Wealth** – Any solution should create incentives for US expats to return and bring back their tax base, investment capital and the jobs that capital creates.

12. **Bring in Foreign Investment** – The solution should create a tax environment that will encourage foreign companies to build plants and factories in the USA.

13. **Revenue Neutral** – The revenue from any reform of the tax code should produce the same revenue as the current system.

These are just the major targets that would define success in a tax reform package. There may be other advantages that could be achieved. But if we achieve even a significant part of the above targets, we will have achieved great success.

Detailing Success

Let's look at each one of the above targets in more detail.

1. Clear and Simple –

The current tax code has become so convoluted that no single person can understand the whole thing. In fact, according to the CCH Standard Tax Reporter, the US tax code would take 72,536 pages to print[14], as of 2011. But if you include all of the ancillary documentation, decisions and judgments that affect how the code is interpreted, it is estimated that it would fill one and a half large 18-wheel trailers.

Even the IRS has to have specialists in each of the various parts of the tax code. But apparently, even those specialists don't always understand the tax code, since the IRS is well known to often give taxpayers incorrect information.

There is a fundamental doctrine in English Common Law, upon which all of our laws are based, that states, ***"Ignorance of the law is no excuse."*** However, our current convoluted tax code makes it impossible for any taxpayer or even any single tax accountant to understand all of our tax laws. It follows then, that if "ignorance of the law is no excuse" and no single

---

[14] Pages Required to Print the US Income Tax Code, The CCH Standard Tax Reporter, 2011,
http://www.cch.com/wbot2011/WBOT_TaxLawPileUp_(28)_f.pdf

person can comprehend our tax code, then the code is far too complex.

Therefore, any reform of the tax code must be simple enough that it would allow an ordinary person, without an accounting degree, to fully understand the law that he is expected to understand and obey.

2. Transparent –

Today's tax system hides large portions of the taxes that everyone pays, from ordinary taxpayers. Most people don't even think about withholding or what it represents in real dollars out of their pockets. But even among those who do, few of them ever really look at their pay stubs and think about things like the employee and employer portions of the payroll tax.

But there are other hidden taxes. Most people don't think of how much they're paying the government, in embedded corporate taxes, every time they buy a shirt, a television, a car, shoes or any other new product. Even the desperately poor, who mistakenly think that they don't pay any tax at all, actually pay a significant amount of tax in every retail purchase they make, including basic cost-of-living items like food, not paid for with food stamps.

Dr. Dale Jorgenson, the former Chairman of the Economics Department at Harvard University, estimated, in a 1996 report[15], that 20% to 30% of the

---

[15] Jorgenson, Dale W., "The Economic Impact of the National Retail Sales Tax," unpublished report sent to Americans for Fair Taxation, November 25, 1996 (since this report is unpublished, there is no download link available)

retail price of most purchases in the USA is made up of embedded income tax and related costs. However, that was an unpublished report to Americans For Fair Taxation, as a part of a larger study. As such, it included data and assumptions that made it less than appropriate in general discussion of this subject.

I mention this study, only because many other people refer to it as factual, while the actual number, though still significant, is probably lower. But if I didn't mention it, then there would be those who would claim that I had failed to consider it. So I mention it, so those people will know that I did look at it.

It contained data beyond just federal taxes and used unrealistic assumptions meant to provide a stable base for the rest of the report. Such special case scenarios are common with interim studies. It seems obvious to me that this particular study was not meant to be a final statement on the subject of embedded income taxes. Therefore, I had to look elsewhere.

What I found was a 2006 report by Arduin, Laffer & Moore Econometrics[16] (Arthur Laffer, by the way, is the creator of the well known Laffer Curve). They took a very conservative approach and estimated the amount of embedded federal income tax in most retail purchases in the USA to be about 10.36%. That includes corporate income taxes and the employer's portion of the payroll tax, but excludes state taxes, which the Jorgenson study

---

[16] Arduin, Laffer & Moore Econometrics, "A Macroeconomic Analysis of the Fairtax Proposal," July 2006
http://www.fairtax.org/PDF/MacroeconomicAnalysisofFairTax.pdf
Note: Again I suggest that you decide how much you trust the source, which is Donna Arduin, Dr. Arthur Laffer, and Stephen Moore.

did not exclude. There are economists who take issue with this study, as well, making arguments that their number is too low. I personally think that it's somewhere in between.

But whichever report you choose to believe, the important thing to remember is that companies don't pay tax, they pass all taxes on to the consumer and that makes the corporate income tax not transparent.

3. Un-Intrusive –

Another of the problems with the current income tax system is how intrusive it has become. It gives the government an open door into the private financial affairs of every US taxpayer. Even though a person has done nothing wrong, a random IRS audit can turn the lives of ordinary, law-abiding people upside down, even when the IRS ultimately finds that they have done nothing wrong. But even worse, the IRS has no effective oversight.

It follows then, that to stop these abuses, any effective tax reform must get the government out of the private financial affairs of citizens.

4. Fair to All –

One of the major problems with the current tax system is that it plays favorites. Worse, its structure is ideal for such favoritism. Both parties give tax breaks to their big donors, while expecting their constituents to pay for those tax breaks. This isn't just Democrats or just Republicans. Both parties have become very adept at pandering and payback, using the IRS tax code as their economic volleyball.

A proper tax reform concept will treat all taxpayers exactly the same, regardless of who they are, whom they may know or how much they donated to a political campaign. In fact, an ideal tax reform concept would make it very difficult, if not impossible, for Congress to play favorites.

5. Un-Tax the Cost-of-Living –

It has long been an accepted premise that the poor should be given some sort of preferential tax treatment to insure that they will not be obligated to pay tax on money that they require for basic cost-of-living purchases (food, rent, electricity, etc.).

Therefore, any tax reform should not place a tax burden on those who are desperately poor.

This isn't to say that the poor should be treated differently. Remember, we want to come up with a tax plan that will treat everyone the same. This makes un-taxing the cost-of-living, while treating everyone the same, a challenge to overcome.

6. Increase Compliance –

There are people at all income levels who dodge taxes. In 2009, the U.S. Department of the Treasury reported that the Gross Tax Gap was $450 billion[17]. After enforcement actions and late payments were taken into account the Tax Gap dropped by $65 billion, leaving a Net Tax Gap of to $385 billion.

---

[17] "IRS Releases New Tax Gap Estimates", Jan. 6, 2012, http://www.irs.gov/newsroom/article/0,,id=252038,00.html

The Gross Tax Gap is defined as, the difference between the amount of tax that taxpayers legally owe the government and the amount that is actually paid voluntarily and on time. The Net Tax Gap is defined as that portion of the Gross Tax Gap that is **never recovered**.

Therefore, if possible, any tax reform plan should increase compliance and reduce both the Gross Tax Gap and the Net Tax Gap.

7. Reduce Compliance Costs –

Depending on which economist you listen to, it costs Americans between $350 billion and $450 billion to comply with the current tax code, each year. Some of that is personal costs, but most is corporate costs that are passed on to the consumer. In the end, complying with the current tax code costs the average taxpayer over $1000 a year in their own costs, plus embedded corporate compliance costs, in the price of items they buy.

8. Reward Savings and Investment –

One of the major problems with our current system is that it's regressive. It effectively punishes savings and investments, while rewarding spending. Of course, now that I think about it, our elected officials like spending **our** money so much, that I suppose that we shouldn't be surprised that they want us to spend what they haven't spent, of our money.

However, the problem with rewarding spending, is that you are building a society that will have little or no money when they retire and will need government support. But then again, that may be what they want.

Any effective tax reform will reward savings and investment.

9. Tax the Underground Economy –

Under our current tax system, the people who deserve to be taxed most, because they cost us so much in government services, pay almost no federal income tax. Drug dealers, auto thieves, burglars, prostitutes, and illegal aliens are just a few of the dregs of society who most cost those of us who pay taxes.

If a way can be found to tax the underground economy, then it should be part of our tax reform package.

10. Repatriate Off-Shored Jobs –

A good part of the incentive for US companies to send jobs to other countries is lower salaries in those countries. But that's just part of their incentive. There are also huge tax incentives for sending jobs offshore.

While we can't do anything about the low salaries in other countries, we can create tax incentives for staying in the USA or returning. This should be a major part of any tax reform package.

11. Repatriate Lost Wealth –

As discussed in Part 2, many of our most financially prolific taxpayers have been leaving the USA and taking all of their wealth with them. This of course means that the jobs that their wealth used to fund have now moved offshore. And let us not forget that we need those wealthy people to pay taxes, so the whole load doesn't fall on those who are left.

Whatever tax reform we come up with must offer incentives for the wealthiest to return, with their hefty check books in tow.

12. Bring in Foreign Investment –

When foreign capital is invested in the USA, it creates more jobs in the USA. But today, our tax system is driving foreign investors to look for other countries where they can invest at a higher profit and with less government intervention.

A good tax reform system will offer advantages to foreign companies to invest in the USA. The same incentives that encourage repatriation of lost wealth may help bring in foreign investment. However, since these investors have no past association with the USA, the incentives may need to be stronger.

13. Revenue Neutral –

Last, but not least, a viable tax reform system will provide the same amount of tax collections to government, as the current system. We can talk about reducing spending. But even if we do reduce spending, we still have a deficit to make up.

A well-crafted tax reform system must be revenue neutral.

12. Crafting a Solution

In the last chapter, we set a rather ambitious set of goals. Of course, as stated earlier, these goals are established to tell us how successful we've been. Even if we don't achieve all of them, if we achieve a large part of them, then we will have been very successful.

I must admit that several years ago, when I first realized what damage the current tax code was doing to our country, I quickly became a fan of the Flat Income Tax. But then I sat down and created a list of goals, very similar to the one above and I soon realized that the Flat Income Tax would meet but a few of the criteria that would define success. There had to be a better answer. There was.

Fortunately, a few years earlier, in 1994, three Houston businessmen had decided to attack this problem and put up their own money to have the best economic minds in the country work on the problem.

Jack Trotter, Bob McNair, and Leo Linbeck were having lunch in Houston in 1994 and they got to talking about what kind of lasting legacy they would leave behind. (Note: Bob McNair owns the NFL team, The Houston Texans.)

So they came upon one problem that they all agreed needed to be addressed and that nobody was currently addressing with any degree of success. Ultimately, each of the three men pledged $1.5 million, of their own money, as seed capital to hire tax and economics experts to identify the real faults with the current tax system, determine what American citizens would like to see in tax reform, and then to design the best and fairest system of taxation, to address those points.

A few months later, in 1995, Americans for Fair Taxation[18] (AFFT) was created. AFFT went on to raise an additional $17 million in the short term. They have now spent more than $23 million to fund focus groups with citizens around the country and numerous tax policy studies with top economists.

What this all boils down to is that their ultimate solution is by far the most thoroughly researched and vetted tax reform proposal in history.

AFFT hired some of the best economists, tax experts, and pollsters in the country, to solve this problem. But most importantly, they didn't tell those experts that they wanted them to justify any particular type of tax reform. Instead, as mentioned above, they were to base whatever tax system they came up with on what faults **they** found with the current system and what **their** surveys determined **Americans** wanted. They received no instruction from any of the three businessmen, other than to create the best and fairest possible solution.

The initial studies that were expected to take up to two years ended up taking almost five years. Only after determining 1) the real problems and 2) the goals for a tax system that would best serve all Americans, they set about designing a workable solution. (Remember

---

[18] Americans For Fair Taxation, Houston TX, http://fairtax.org/

problem solving 101, where you first define the problem and what goals constitute success?)

In the end, they called their solution, the **FairTax**.

They provided volumes of research and documentation to Congress and the media. In short order, the FairTax got the attention of members of Congress. In 1999, it was introduced as bills in both houses. As more congressmen come to understand the benefits of the FairTax, it gathers more co-sponsors, crossing party lines. It is now championed by 76 current members of Congress and has been in the platform of three former presidential candidates – two Republican and one Democrat.

Today, the FairTax exists in the House as H.R.25[19] and in the Senate as S.13[20]. It has even been heard by the House Ways and Means Committee. However, establishment members of both parties have thus far blocked it from coming to the Floor of the House. I can only assume that the leadership doesn't want to give up the power that the current tax system gives them (tax breaks for political donations, etc.).

However, with each new Congress, the FairTax gains more new supporters. In fact, many of the TEA Party candidates are supporters of the FairTax. What this means is that the establishment won't be able to bottle it up in committee much longer.

---

[19] The FairTax Act of 2011 (House version)
http://thomas.loc.gov/cgi-bin/bdquery/z?d112:H.R.25:

[20] The FairTax Act of 2011 (Senate version)
http://thomas.loc.gov/cgi-bin/bdquery/z?d112:S.13:

Co-sponsors and supporters of the FairTax include former presidential candidates Rep. Duncan Hunter (R-CA), Gov. Mike Huckabee (R-AK), and Sen. Mike Gravel (D-AK). Even Herman Cain supported the FairTax, before he came up with his "9-9-9" plan. The FairTax sponsors are Sen. Saxby Chambliss (GA) and Rep. Rob Woodall (GA). I won't list all of the co-sponsors here. But just a few of the key co-sponsors of the FairTax include, Sen. Jim DeMint (SC), Sen. Richard Lugar (IN), Rep. Darrell Issa (CA), Rep. Mike Pence (IN) and Rep. Ted Poe (TX). There are 76 sponsors and co-sponsors, in all.

But enough of how the FairTax came to be and who is behind it. Let's look at what makes it the only viable solution that exists as a bill in Congress today.

13. A Bill That Fills the Bill

- Make April 15 just another day.

- Never again fear opening a letter from the IRS.

- Keep 100% of your paycheck.

Those are just a few of the benefits of the FairTax.

The economists who were charged with finding a viable and equitable "fix" for our tax system quickly came to the conclusion that there was no way to "fix" the current income tax. That's because it was flawed from the start. There is just no way to make a tax on income achieve even a few of the goals that they had set. It would have to be completely replaced.

That's why the FairTax is a complete tax reform package that doesn't just tinker around the edges of the current system and adjust marginal tax rates, but instead, completely replaces every vestige of the income tax and IRS. That's right. Even the IRS would go away and be replaced with a much smaller agency that would deal only with the states. Instead of 140,000 IRS agents, dealing with 138 million taxpayers, there would be maybe 25 auditors for each state, dealing only with that state.

In short, the FairTax is a comprehensive, revenue neutral proposal that replaces all federal income and payroll based taxes with a progressive national retail sales tax and ensures that no American pays federal taxes on spending up to the poverty level. Companion legislation offers an amendment to the Constitution that would repeal the 16th Amendment.

The FairTax abolishes and replaces all federal personal and corporate income taxes, gift taxes, the "death tax," capital gains taxes, alternative minimum taxes, and self-employment taxes. It also replaces Social Security contributions and Medicare taxes. In fact, every item that is represented on your current form 1040, is replaced with one simple, visible, national retail sales tax, collected only at the point of final retail sale of new items and services. Better yet, it is administered primarily by existing state sales tax authorities (only 5 states don't already have sales tax collection agencies in place).

At this time, I want to make one point perfectly clear. Many of the tax and spend opponents of the FairTax try to mislead the public into thinking that the FairTax is a Value Added Tax (VAT), such as is found in Europe. Well here's the truth. If you read the bill, you'll know this to be factual.

The FairTax is <u>NOT</u> a VAT!

Here's the difference. A VAT is collected at every point along the manufacturing and distribution chain, where value is added. The FairTax, by contrast, is collected **ONLY** at the point of final retail sale. There is a big difference, not the least of which, are complexity (remember that Goal 1 is simplicity) and compliance costs (Goal 7).

That's why the FairTax is a **"retail"** sales tax, instead of a VAT. Remember that a VAT has not worked in Europe. It will not work in the USA. In fact, a VAT fails on more than half of our goals.

Here's how the FairTax works.

1. The FairTax abolishes the income tax (personal and corporate), employment taxes, and the IRS and it replaces them all with a single rate national retail sales tax, collected only at the point of final retail sale of new products or services.

2. That means that there is no withholding, no alternative minimum tax, no inheritance tax, no gift tax, no capital gains tax and no audits. Everything that was covered in your withholding is shifted into that national retail sales tax.

3. A "prebate" (rebate in advance) will eliminate taxes on spending up to the poverty line, thus un-taxing cost-of-living expenses. The prebate will be based on family size and will be equal to the amount of FairTax that would be paid on new retail purchases of products and services with a total retail cost equal to the poverty level for a family of that size.

4. The FairTax rate is 23%, though very few people will pay at that rate, due to the prebate. A family of 4, for example, spending at around $50,000 per year will effectively pay around 8% in FairTax.

5. The states - not the federal government - will collect the FairTax from retail businesses and the states – not the federal government - will be responsible for insuring compliance. 45 of the 50 states already

collect a sales tax and thus, have the infrastructure in place for such sales tax collections and compliance audits. A small portion of the FairTax will be withheld by the states as payment for these collection services.

But one of the most important advantages to the FairTax is not in how it functions, but rather, that it turns the USA into a tremendous investment and jobs magnet. Here's how it works.

1. It would cost less to produce products in the USA than in any other producer nation because the USA would be the only producer nation in the world without a corporate income tax.

2. US-sourced products would therefore be priced lower, both at wholesale and retail, whether in the USA or abroad.

3. Lower prices for US-sourced products would mean more sales of US products.

4. More sales of US products would require more production capability in the USA, to handle the increased demand for US products.

5. Of course, more production facilities would mean more US jobs.

It's a win-win-win situation.

More jobs are created in the USA, the companies sell more products, and the US economy gets stronger.

14. Evaluating Success

Speaking of goals, let's look at how the FairTax addresses the goals that were set earlier. Remember that we don't have to achieve all of those goals, since those goals were designed only as a measurement tool, not as absolute requirements. By that, I mean that we can measure the success of any tax proposal by how many of those goals we achieve.

So let's see how close we can get to fulfilling each of those goals.

1. Clear and Simple –

Compliance with the FairTax is beyond simple, for both the customer and the business.

It's collected by businesses, at the point of every retail purchase of a new product or service, *without the help of an accountant.*

There would be no complex corporate income tax forms for the business collecting the tax to fill out. In place of those complex income tax forms, would be a single short form that simply reports the total sales and calculates 23% of that amount as sales tax. It doesn't get much easier than that. Well... actually, it does.

You see, since the vast majority of retail businesses use some sort of electronic cash register or billing software, all that would be required of those businesses, would be to update their cash register or billing software. No accountants required.

But it gets even better. In 45 of the 50 states, the structure for collecting and remitting sales tax is <u>already in place</u>; so only five states would have to set up a new collection method to handle the FairTax.

No accountants. No complex forms. No convoluted calculations. Just a flat percentage of every sale.

Clear and Simple?... ☑

2. Transparent –

Under the FairTax, the taxpayer will see every penny that he is paying in FairTax on the purchase receipt or invoice. You can't get any more transparent than that.

Transparent?... ☑

3. Fair to ALL –

Under the FairTax, not only is every taxpayer treated exactly the same, but a sales tax makes it extremely difficult for Congress to play favorites, due to its transparency.

Under the FairTax, every taxpayer pays the exact same 23% sales tax on every retail sale of a new product or payment for a service and every taxpayer receives the exact same cost-of-living prebate, based on family size.

You can't get any more fair than treating every taxpayer exactly the same.

Fair to ALL?... ☑

4. Un-Intrusive –

The FairTax gets the federal government completely out of the financial affairs of individuals. This means no more IRS audits – no more IRS demands for personal financial records – and no more federal window into your personal financial affairs.

This would be true for businesses, as well. Since the FairTax would be collected by the states, the businesses would only be responsible to state authorities. Of course, all businesses are already responsible to state authorities, in some manner, in every state and for sales taxes in 45 states.

The FairTax completely eliminates the federal window into both our personal and business finances. This doesn't mean that they can't still subpoena records, in the case of a criminal investigation. It just means that they can't browse through your personal or business records, without a court order.

Un-Intrusive?... ☑

5. Un-Tax the Cost-of-Living –

The FairTax monthly *"prebate"* is equal to the amount that a taxpayer would pay in FairTax, in one month, for new retail purchases, with a total retail cost equaling the poverty level for a family of his size. This effectively zeroes out all cost-of-living expenses for every taxpayer, from the poorest welfare recipient to the richest billionaire.

Some say that the rich should not receive the cost-of-living prebate. But remember, it's largely the unfairness of the current system that is causing wealth to flee the USA and that's the reason for goal 3 – Fair to ALL. Regardless of what income level you cut off such payments, somebody will complain. Besides, the cost of sending around $600 to each of 400 billionaires is such a small amount, in comparison to the overall budget, that accounting rounding errors could be larger. It's not an issue.

Un-Taxing the Cost-of-living?... ☑

6. Increase Compliance –

If nothing else, simply reducing the number of tax collections points will mean more compliance.

With the income tax, there are 138 million personal income tax filers and 10.5 million business filers[21] for a total of more than 148 million collection points, meaning 148 million chances for cheating.

By contrast, under the FairTax, 138 million of those collection points go away, since the FairTax is collected only at the point of final retail sale (i.e. at a business).

---

[21] IRS Research, Analysis, and Statistics, Office of Research, "Number of Returns Filed, by Type of Return, Fiscal Years 2008 and 2009", July 28, 2010, http://www.irs.gov/pub/irs-soi/09db02nr.xls

But then consider that of those 10.5 million businesses, many are manufacturers and suppliers that have no retail operations, so many of those 10.5 million businesses would not be tax collection points, either. The actual number of tax collection points will be much less than that.

But for argument sake, let's just be generous and go with the 10.5 million number. After all, just knowing that we're using an inflated number that should hurt our argument, to demonstrate how compliance will be increased under the FairTax, only shows how strong the FairTax really is.

So if we reduce the number of tax collection points to just 10.5 million, that represents roughly 7% of the original number of collection points. That means that there will be only 7% as many opportunities for tax evasion under the FairTax as under the income tax and only 7% as many collection points for state (not federal) authorities to monitor. To put it another way, for tax evasion to remain at the same level, under the FairTax, as under the current income tax, the percentage of people evading tax payment would have to increase 14 times more than under the income tax system.

But in fact, the FairTax removes much of the incentive for tax evasion. That means that the percentage of tax evaders would likely go down and would certainly not increase 14 times.

So while there will always be those who will try to cheat on their taxes, the FairTax significantly reduces the number of collection points, where cheating can occur and removes much of the incentive for cheating.

Ultimately, compliance with the FairTax will reflect a significant increase in compliance over the current income tax.

Increase Compliance?... ☑

7. Reduce Compliance Costs –

Under the FairTax, the only place where there are any compliance costs, whatsoever, is at the point of retail sales of a new product or service and even that cost is dramatically reduced from the compliance costs of the corporate income tax. Compliance is simply multiplying total sales by 23% and submitting that amount to the state. The state takes out their portion and submits the rest to the federal government.

Reduce Compliance Costs... ☑

8. Reward Savings and Investment –

The current income tax is regressive, since it punishes savings and investment. Under any system based on the taxation of income, be it flat or progressive, there is no encouragement to invest your money since it is taxed *before* you even have the chance to decide whether to spend or invest it. In fact, if you invest your money, it's taxed again.

The FairTax rewards savings and investment, by taxing only spending, not savings and investment. If you choose to invest a portion of your earnings, rather than spending it, you pay no taxes on it till you decide to cash in your investment and *spend* it. Allowing your savings to accumulate faster is the reward.

Reward Savings and Investment... ☑

9. Tax the Underground Economy –

Every year, billions of dollars in tax revenue is lost to the underground economy. Drug dealers, bookies, burglars, pimps, car thieves, and illegal aliens are just a small portion of the underground economy that pay little or no income tax. But the FairTax collects tax from those people and more, every time they buy a new shirt, get their car repaired or have a beer at the bar.

Even mob bosses will pay tax on their expensive cars and yachts.

Tax the Underground Economy... ☑

10. Repatriate Off-Shored Jobs –

There are two reasons why companies send jobs offshore. One is to save on wages and the other is to save on taxes. The FairTax actually addresses both of these issues, since part of wages is the employer portion of the payroll tax.

Wages – While wages in other countries will remain lower than US wages, the FairTax eliminates the payroll tax, which will reduce how much it costs US employers to keep an employee on the payroll in the USA. But the decision on whether or not to move jobs offshore is based on many factors, including shipping costs and insurance. A small change can make a big difference in whether or not it's worthwhile to have those jobs offshore. Reducing the wage differential, even a little bit, could be a big step in that direction.

Taxes – When companies move jobs offshore, they most often create offshore corporations, to handle those jobs. Those offshore companies give them tax benefits, back in the USA. However, since there is a corporate income tax in every other major nation, the lack of an income tax in the USA moves the tax benefit back to the USA.

The FairTax will create a huge incentive for American companies to return jobs to the USA.

Repatriate Off-Shored Jobs... ☑

11. Repatriate Lost Wealth –

One of the primary reasons why so many wealthy Americans are fleeing the USA is that they feel like they are being punished for being successful and the vehicle for that punishment is the current income tax system and the IRS. But wherever they go, they still end up paying some income tax – just not at the punitive levels that they paid in the USA. Other nations also don't have overly aggressive tax agencies, looking into their every transaction.

The FairTax eliminates the entire income tax system, including the agency that those wealthy expats saw as a threat. Suddenly, those "taxpatriates", as they call themselves, will find that they are paying income tax on their profits, in their new nation, while such tax is not collected back in the USA.

Now in reality, some of those expats will not return, since they will have settled in their new nation, have friends there and have adapted to the climate. Those few will not see the changes in the US tax law as enough to make them want to move again.

But most will see the FairTax as a huge enticement to return, with their overflowing checkbooks in tow, since it means that their investments will grow faster in the USA, without a regressive tax on income.

Repatriate Lost Wealth... ☑

12. Bring in Foreign Investment –

As discussed earlier, foreign corporations would have a great incentive, under the FairTax, to produce their products in the USA.

Although there are nations like Bahamas, Cape Verde and Gibraltar that have little or no corporate income tax, those nations generally have no manufacturing base. The nations with populations to support a manufacturing base, such as Japan, Mexico, Korea and Germany, to name but a few, have corporate income taxes in the 25 to 35 percent range.

So if those foreign companies could do their manufacturing in the USA, where their production costs would contain no income tax component, it would represent a 25 to 35 percent cost savings that they could use to make their US-manufactured products more competitive around the world.

By this I mean that the lower production costs would allow them to sell their "Made in USA" quality products at a lower price, while making more profit at that lower price. The lower price, in turn, would mean that their products would be more competitive in the world market and that would drive up their sales. More sales and more profit per sale is an irresistible draw.

The FairTax would, by eliminating the income tax component of production costs, create a huge magnet for foreign investment.

Bring in Foreign Investment... ☑

13. Revenue Neutral –

Whatever changes we make to the tax code, it must be revenue neutral. When I talk to groups about the FairTax, there are always those who say that we should cut both spending and taxes. Certainly, it would be nice to be able to cut spending. I think we should. But that's a completely different issue. Although taxes and spending are joined at the hip, they are two different issues.

We have to approach any changes to the tax code as though nothing else will change. If spending is eventually cut, then we can decide what to do with the tax rates of whatever tax system we have at that time. But for now, we must assume that spending levels will remain static.

As mentioned earlier, the FairTax is the most thoroughly researched and vetted tax reform package in US history. Over $23 million has been spent, hiring many of the very best economists and tax experts in the nation and conducting market studies and focus groups. The FairTax was not an idea that these experts had to justify, but a solution that these experts designed to fit the needs of our nation.

The number one priority with which these top experts were charged was that whatever they came up with, it had to be revenue neutral. I have to believe that with so many great economic minds focused on this issue, revenue neutrality is insured.

Revenue Neutral... ☑

There have been a few economists claim that at 23%, the FairTax would not be revenue neutral. But all of them are basing their claims on limited data and pre-conceived notions that do not apply.

Remember back in the beginning of this book, I suggested that you know your source. Well here's where it really comes into play.

I'm not an economist. But then, I'm not the source.

As a researcher, what I've learned from researching the FairTax, is that Americans For Fair Taxation hired the best available economists, tax experts, pollsters, and other professionals. They provided those experts with the funding necessary to be able to do their jobs, with certainty. In other words, they didn't skimp.

I also listened closely to those who have spoken against the FairTax and I learned that they are basing their opposition to the FairTax on academic, but unproven economic "theory" or under-funded studies that were limited in scope. Nobody that I have heard speak against the FairTax has based their comments on studies that are even half as detailed and wide-ranging as those that support the FairTax.

It's your decision

You have to make your own decision. The purpose of this book is not to detail the economics of the FairTax. Rather, it's to make you aware of hidden problems with the income tax and to provide you with a general introduction to the FairTax and how it will benefit ALL Americans, across the board.

My purpose is not to provide you with all the answers, because I don't know which questions are most important to you. Rather, my purpose is to point you in the right direction, give you a few starting points (i.e. all of the links provided in the footnotes and near the end of Chapter 3) and the tools necessary to answer all of the questions for yourself.

I've provided you with several good sources where you can find your own answers. Just remember to always verify and judge the source, not the messenger.

By using the tools and links that I have provided, doing your own research should not be all that time consuming. I encourage you to do so.

Our current tax system and Washington, DC's *"Soak the Rich"* mentality, which the income tax enables, is largely responsible for driving away millions of our most financially prolific taxpayers, most wealthy investors, most productive citizens and most profuse job creators. These are the people that this nation needs most.

The FairTax is not a magic bullet. But as you can see, it meets all of the goals that are required of a good tax reform package.

Once again, I strongly encourage you to use the links provided and do your own research. I'm sure that if you do, you'll agree that most of the issues discussed herein and more can be resolved with the FairTax.

But whatever you ultimately decide, just remember that our convoluted tax system is one of the primary motivations driving away the innovators, the risk takers, those who pay the lion's share of taxes and create the lion's share of jobs. If we allow the government to continue to use our tax system to punish success, this flight will continue and increase. As more of the wealthy are driven away, their share of the tax load will fall increasingly and disproportionately on lower income groups.

Whether or not you believe the FairTax to be the perfect solution, there is at least one solution that is fair to all and will not only help prevent further "taxpatriation," but that will actually draw wealth and jobs back to the USA. I've said all that I can say to paint an accurate picture of the problem that is facing us today and provided you with the best sources of information available to the general public. I hope that you'll agree that I've presented a sound and thoroughly researched solution.

So I would like to leave you with just one final thought.

Remember what happens if we keep driving wealth offshore...